NATURAL SOLUTIONS
for
CLEANING & WELLNESS

HALLE COTTIS

Holistic Life Coach & founder of
Whole Lifestyle Nutrition

PAGE STREET
PUBLISHING CO.

PAGE STREET
PUBLISHING CO.

First published in 2017 by
Page Street Publishing Co.
27 Congress Street, Suite 105
Salem, MA 01970
www.pagestreetpublishing.com

Distributed by Macmillan, sales in Canada by The Canadian Manda Group.

19 18 17 16   1 2 3 4 5

ISBN-13: 978-1-62414-323-6
ISBN-10: 1-62414-323-7

Library of Congress Control Number: 2016948529

Cover and book design by Page Street Publishing Co.
Woodcarvings by Carla Bauer.
All photographs are from Shutterstock, except for pages 25, 27, 40, 54, 68, 72, 74, 80, 86, 108, 117, 118, 126, 141 and 142 which are from Depositphoto; pages 73 and 167, which are by Halle Cottis; and page 188 which is by Lauren Lawson.

Printed and bound in China

Page Street is proud to be a member of 1% for the Planet. Members donate one percent of their sales to one or more of the over 1,500 environmental and sustainability charities across the globe who participate in this program.

TO MY GIRLS, AUBREE, BRYNN
AND KENNA. THIS BOOK'S FOR YOU,
GIRLS. AND TO MY HUSBAND, DAVID.
YOUR UNCONDITIONAL SUPPORT AND
GUIDANCE HAVE ALWAYS KEPT
ME BELIEVING IN MYSELF.
WE'VE GOT THIS!

CONTENTS

Introduction 9

Get to Know Your Natural Ingredients—The Basics 11

NATURAL SOLUTIONS FOR THE HOME 21

BATHROOM 23

Toilet Cleaner 24

Soft Scrub Bathtub, Shower and Sink Cleaner 25

Mold and Mildew Cleaner 26

Soap Scum Cleaner 27

Scouring Powder 28

Grout Cleaner 29

Hard Water Deposit Remover 30

Mirror Cleaner 31

KITCHEN 33

Lemon Dish Soap 34

Powdered Dishwasher Detergent and Rinse Aid 35

All-Purpose Disinfectant Cleaner 36

Stainless Steel Cleaner 37

Granite Countertop Cleaner 38

Degreaser 39

Eliminate Sponge Odor 39

Microwave Oven Cleaner 40

Oven Cleaner 41

Garbage Disposal Cleaner 41

Drain Clog Remover 42

Coffee Pot and Coffee Machine Cleaner 43
Cast Iron Skillet Cleaner 44
Silver and Tarnish Cleaner 45
Solid Copper Cleaner 46
Cutting Board Cleaner 47

LAUNDRY 49

Powder Laundry Detergent 50
Liquid Laundry Detergent 51
Lemon Bleach Alternative 51
Scented Fabric Softener 52
Washing Machine Deodorizer 53
Sour Towel Relief 54
Blood Stain Remover 55
Laundry Stain Remover 55

HOUSEHOLD CLEANING 57

Streak-Free Window Cleaner
(Indoor and Outdoor) 58
General Floor Cleaner 59
Wood Floor Cleaner 60
Label and Sticky Residue Remover 60
Carpet Stain Remover (Wet and Dry) 61
Cigarette Smoke Odor Remover 62
Fabric Upholstery Freshener 63
Fresh-Cut Flower Food 64
Crayon and Pencil Mark Remover for Walls 65
Leather Furniture Cleaner and Conditioner 66
Electronic and Television Screen Cleaner 67

FRESHENERS AND DEODORIZERS 69

Carpet Deodorizer 70
Air Freshener Spray 71
Bathroom Air Freshener 72
No-Wax Candles 73
Simmering Potpourri 74
Refrigerator Deodorizer 75
Trash Can Deodorizer 76
Car Deodorizer 77
Fish and Bacon Odor Remover 78
Odor Remover (for Garlic and
Onion on Hands) 79

PEST CONTROL 81

Asian Lady Beetles 82
Asian Lady Beetles: Eliminate Their Scent 83
Cockroaches 84
Fleas 85
Fruit Flies 86
Ant Control 87
Bed Bugs 88
Hornets and Wasps 89
Centipedes and Millipedes 90
Mice 91

OUTDOORS 93

Bug Spray and Patio Diffuser Repellent 94
Weed Killer 95
Natural Garden Pesticide 96
Heavy-Duty Grill Cleaner 97
Screen Cleaner 97
Car Wash Soap 98
Wax for Cars 98
Car De-Icer 99

NATURAL SOLUTIONS FOR COMMON HEALTH PROBLEMS 101

HEAD, EARS, FACE AND MOUTH 103

Headaches and Migraines 104
Healing and Nourishing Customizable Dry Shampoo 105
All-Natural Head Lice Treatment 106
Nourishing Hair Mask 107
Lighten Hair Naturally 108
Darken Hair Naturally 109
Dandruff Control 110
Stye 111
Pinkeye 112

Excess Wax Removal from Ears 113
Swimmer's Ear 114
Gingivitis 115
Toothache Relief 116
Whitening Teeth 117
Remineralizing Peppermint or Cinnamon Toothpaste 118
Bad Breath Control and Mouthwash 119
Canker Sores 120
Cold Sores 121
Healing Lip Balm 122
Allergies 123
Foaming Face Wash and Toner 124
Acne Control Mask 125

CHEST, THROAT AND IMMUNE SYSTEM 127

Nasal Decongestant Rinse 128
Cough and Sore Throat Syrup 129
Vapor Rub 130
Flu 132
Heartburn, Acid Reflux and GERD 133
Stomachache 134
Restoring Electrolytes 135

HANDS, LEGS, ARMS AND FEET 137

Foaming Hand Wash 138
Sensitive Skin Body Wash 138
Hand Sanitizer 139
Easy Deodorant Spray 140
Sensitive Skin Deodorant Cream 141
Creamy Lotion 142
Sunscreen 143
Foot Odor 144
Athlete's Foot 145
Jock Itch 146
Healing Balm (for Sore Muscles and Joint Pain) 147

SKIN IRRITATIONS AND HEALTH CONDITIONS 149

Eczema Treatment 150
Plaque Psoriasis Treatment 151
Rosacea Treatment 152
Soothing Rosacea Gel 153
Minor Skin Burns 154
Minor Cut Disinfectant and Healing Ointment 155
Bruises 156
Razor Bumps 157
Warts 158
Splinters 159
Chafing Powder 160

Poison Ivy and Poison Oak 161
Bee and Wasp Stings 162
Anti-Itch Bug Bite Lotion 163
Flexible, Reusable Ice Packs 164
Reusable Heating Pads 165
Do-It-Yourself Adhesive Bandages 166
Butterfly Adhesive Bandages (to help close a wound) 167

DIGESTIVE SYSTEM 169

Constipation 170
Diarrhea 171
Healing Drink for Diarrhea 171
Hemorrhoids 172
Gas, Bloating and Belching 173
Hiccups 175

EMOTIONAL AND PAIN SUPPORT 177

PMS and Menstrual Cramps 178
Nature's Pain Relief 180
Detox Bath 181
Seasonal Depression 182
Insomnia 183
Anxiety 185

References 186
Acknowledgments 188
About the Author 188
Index 189

INTRODUCTION

I grew up in the rural hillsides of Holmes County, Ohio, where the Amish still live and the charm of how things once were done is still present.

Both my parents were from the city and had moved to the countryside for a simpler lifestyle.

While I was growing up, my mom used cloth diapers, grew her own herb garden and cooked completely from scratch. My father successfully ran a thriving egg business.

During our first five years in Holmes County, we lived in a home with an Amish family. What an incredible experience this turned out to be! We helped each other and learned techniques that the Amish follow regularly for a more natural lifestyle.

The Amish pride themselves on doing things without technology or the use of modern amenities. A few examples passed onto us were disinfecting our clothes by hanging them out to line-dry in the sun, naturally bleaching our clothes with some lemon juice and the sun and cleaning the windows with newspapers. We also learned some great gardening tips.

The Amish weren't the only people who influenced us; my grandma did, too! She liked to use natural solutions whenever possible. She taught us to use vinegar on a bee sting to stop the pain. It was her magic potion that stopped our stomachs from hurting. Her natural techniques and love greatly influenced how I grew up.

I went off to college. Being the independent person that I am, I thought the modern amenities presented in front of me were the way things should be done from this point on. I adopted some lifestyle choices that were really bad for my health and my environment.

After college, I married; and in 19 months I went from having zero kids to three girls. It's funny how quickly life can change. I still thought that my so-called new and improved ways of doing things were safer and easier, even though I was using chemicals. Everything changed when one of my crawling babies made her way over to a bucket of cleaning solution on the floor and stuck her hands in it. I gasped. It happened in a split second! Since I didn't know whether she'd put her hands in her mouth, I immediately contacted Poison Control. Thankfully, she was okay, but from that moment, my attitude changed.

(continued)

I had a family now and three beautiful girls to protect, so my decisions affected all of us. I stuck my nose into the best books out there. I found my way back to my roots and embraced a natural lifestyle once again. I felt good knowing that my girls were crawling on floors without a trace of any chemicals.

I studied up on natural solutions for our health as well. One of my daughters and I suffer from a skin disorder. It was recommended that we live the cleanest and greenest way possible, including the medications that we choose. Once again, this was a change for us. I didn't realize that some medicines prescribed by our doctors could actually be harmful to our health and that there were better alternative healing methods.

Instead of running to the doctor, we soothed our skin disorder with natural creams. I also discovered a natural way to end my 10-year insomnia battle and I even got rid of a chronic ear infection that an ear specialist could not. I was shocked by how effective these solutions were! They often worked better than prescribed medications.

Over the years, I have come up with a great many natural solutions that my family and I have used in our home and for our health. I am honored to share them with you! Here's wishing you and your family good health and happiness.

Halle Cottis

GET TO KNOW YOUR NATURAL INGREDIENTS— THE BASICS

It can seem overwhelming to take the leap from store-bought solutions to all-natural homemade ones. Don't try to change everything all at once. Grow your collection of natural ingredients slowly over time. Take baby steps and keep growing.

Most, if not all, of these ingredients are used in multiple recipes featured in this book. In most cases, only a small amount of each ingredient is needed. This makes your ingredients last a lot longer, which saves you a lot of money over time.

When looking for containers and equipment to make your own solutions, think about recycling what you already have. Reuse an old can or dedicate a mason jar for melting your waxes. Use old ketchup and mustard bottles for squeeze containers. Use an old Parmesan cheese container for ingredients that you sprinkle. Use old t-shirts as cleaning rags. If you're creative, you can recycle all kinds of old or used items.

WHY IS IT IMPORTANT TO LIVE A NATURAL LIFESTYLE?

When you come home from a long day, you want to be able to kick off your shoes, snuggle up on a comfy couch and enjoy a clean and safe environment. You need your home to be your safe haven, a place where you can unwind and fully relax.

The world is full of toxins that can dramatically affect our health and lifestyle. The good news is that you can easily reduce the toxins in your home and health products by replacing several staple ingredients. Sure, it might be a little less convenient to make your own solutions, but it is absolutely necessary for good health and for our environment.

Am I suggesting that you run out right now and buy all the natural ingredients in this book? No. You would be overwhelmed. Big results are achieved with little steps!

When I first started my healthy lifestyle journey, I began slowly by tackling the foods that came into my home. I believe strongly that quality foods and herbs are our best medicines. Over several years, I worked on changing my diet to wholesome healthy foods and I reduced the toxins that I absorbed from foods.

But toxins also come from other sources, more specifically our environment. I felt I had adequate time to tackle my diet and now it was time to move onto my lifestyle changes. Little by little I used more vinegar to clean. I ditched my toxic candles and replaced them with a natural alternative that was safe for myself and our environment. I made my own hand soaps and was incredibly surprised how inexpensive and easy it was. I took it slowly so that I did not get overwhelmed. This is a journey, and journeys are meant to happen over time.

Time matters when we transition into a natural lifestyle. Start slowly. If you are looking to clear your house of toxins, start with one room. Which room do you feel is most important for improving your family's health? Once you feel you've tackled that room like a champ, move on to the next room. Odds are that the natural ingredients you purchased will carry over to the next room, too!

When you start to work on natural solutions for your health, start with your diet. So many health conditions can dramatically improve if we add more quality fruits and vegetables to our diet. If you are trying to heal yourself, eliminate trigger foods such as processed foods, artificial sweeteners, dairy, eggs, wheat, soy and table sugar. Take it one step at a time and recognize that healing takes months, sometimes years, but take comfort in knowing that you are heading in the right direction.

With these positive changes happening, you will start to notice big shifts in your home and your health. Embrace the process every step of the way!

Nature provides us with so many healing and cleaning ingredients such as lemons, coconut oil, lavender, salt and beeswax.

INGREDIENTS FOR NATURAL SOLUTIONS

Get to know your natural ingredients! Here is a list of ingredients featured in this book, each with a brief description and common uses.

ALMOND OIL (SWEET)

Sweet almond oil is a hypoallergenic oil that is often used for the skin, hair and medicinal purposes. It is rich in Vitamin E, fatty acids, magnesium, zinc, potassium, proteins and other vital minerals and vitamins. It is commonly used to cleanse the skin and remove deep circles from under the eyes. It also helps control hair loss.

ALOE VERA (PURE AND ORGANIC)

Pure aloe vera gel comes right from the aloe plant. It has antibacterial qualities and contains vitamins and minerals. If you do not have access to an aloe plant, look for pure aloe vera where you shop. It should be free of any perfumes, dyes and artificial ingredients. Aloe vera has so many uses. It moisturizes skin, tones skin, relieves minor burns and makes an excellent eye makeup remover.

ARROWROOT POWDER (OR STARCH)

Arrowroot starch is a powdery substance that comes from the roots of the plant *Maranta arundinacea*, also called arrowroot. This herb, native to South America, is often found in rain forests. Arrowroot has become a popular grain-free diet option and is used in the kitchen as a thickening agent and for baking. Arrowroot aids digestion, helps heal skin problems, benefits the hair and is used by many as a natural baby powder.

BAKING SODA

Baking soda is a natural chemical compound called sodium bicarbonate. It is used in cooking and cleaning. Baking soda can be used as a deodorizer, antacid, mild disinfectant and fire extinguisher. It's also popular for pest control and personal hygiene.

BEESWAX PELLETS

Beeswax is a natural wax secreted by bees to form honeycombs. Beeswax pellets are little pieces that melt down much more easily than beeswax bars. Beeswax thickens creams and lotions and can be used to make lip balms. It also relieves rashes, and makes great non-toxic candles.

BENTONITE CLAY POWDER

Bentonite clay powder is a powdery substance created of volcanic ash. Pure bentonite clay is great for pulling out metals, toxins and other chemicals. It is great for the skin and for detoxing and removing impurities from the body. It also makes an effective toothpaste.

BORAX

Borax is known as sodium borate or disodium tetraborate. Borax is a mineral salt of boric acid, but it is not the same as boric acid. It is a common ingredient in natural cleaning products, laundry detergents, deodorizers and disinfectants, and it also softens water and cleans floors.

CALCIUM CARBONATE POWDER

Calcium carbonate powder is a chalk-like substance that helps maintain healthy bones and remineralizes teeth. It can be used for heartburn, indigestion and upset stomach.

CASTILE LIQUID SOAP

Castile soap is made from plant oils, typically olive and coconut oil. These oils are mixed with potassium hydroxide to create a natural liquid soap. It is made without foaming agents, harsh cleaners or antibacterial agents and is biodegradable and completely earth-friendly. When using castile soap, do not mix it with vinegar or lemon juice, because they will cancel out its effectiveness. Castile soap is often used for laundry detergent, foaming hand soap and foaming carpet stain remover.

CASTOR OIL

Castor oil is an anti-inflammatory and anti-oxidant, pale yellow oil obtained from castor beans. It has antibacterial components and has a lot of uses within the health field. Castor oil is often used as a laxative and for common skin problems, and can even be used as an all-natural stye treatment.

COCONUT OIL

Coconut oil, from the fruit of the coconut palm tree, has been known to help heal a long list of conditions. It can help with weight loss, thyroid conditions, low energy and IBS (irritable bowel syndrome), among others, and it is an effective natural sunscreen.

COLLOIDAL SILVER

Colloidal silver is a mineral that can be beneficial for the body in many different ways. It has antibacterial, antiviral and anti-inflammatory properties; it helps heal wounds and cuts; and it helps treat eczema, rosacea and psoriasis. Other common uses are as a natural nasal spray and a natural mouthwash. It can even help clear up ear infections.

DIATOMACEOUS EARTH—FOOD GRADE (NOT POOL GRADE)

Diatomaceous earth is a chalk-like substance composed of fossilized diatoms that have formed into silica deposits. The silica deposits are ground into a fine powder called diatomaceous earth. It is most commonly used as a natural insecticide and is great to use on your furry friends to get rid of fleas. There are two different grades of diatomaceous earth: food grade and pool grade. Food-grade diatomaceous earth is safe to use for your home, yards and animals. Pool-grade diatomaceous earth has been altered by high heat and is safe to use only in pools. Be sure to buy food-grade diatomaceous earth for the natural solutions presented in this book.

DISTILLED WHITE VINEGAR

Vinegar is a sour and acidic fermented liquid used to flavor or preserve foods and to clean things. It is inexpensive, non-toxic and biodegradable and is a useful disinfectant. It can be an alternative to bleach and can also soften your laundry. There are many uses for vinegar.

DR. BRONNER'S SAL SUDS

Sometimes you need specific ingredients to create suds. One of those ingredients is sodium lauryl sulfate (SLS), which is not to be confused with sodium laureate sulfate (SLES). These two ingredients are completely different. SLES has been known to contain carcinogens; SLS does not contain carcinogens. Unlike with castile liquid soap, lemon juice and vinegar can be added to Sal Suds with great success. Sal Suds is commonly used as a dish soap, a liquid laundry detergent and a heavy-duty degreaser.

ESSENTIAL OILS

Essential oils are volatile oils that come from the leaves, stems, flowers, bark, roots or other elements of a plant. These oils are distilled by steam, by steam plus water, by plain water or by expression. Essential oils have been known to repel pests and parasites, to provide antibacterial and anti-fungal protection and to have therapeutic effects on the mind, emotions and body.

ETHANOL ALCOHOL

Ethanol alcohol is a drinking alcohol that is found in beer, wine and liquor. It is commonly used in air fresheners and to get rid of strong odors. It can be used as a natural deodorant, to freshen up smelly upholstery and even as a bug repellant.

HYDROGEN PEROXIDE (FOOD GRADE 3%)

Hydrogen peroxide is a colorless liquid with strong oxidizing properties. It is commonly used as a disinfectant and a bleach alternative. It works great as a stain remover, and it cleans grout like nothing else! Hydrogen peroxide can also be used for dental care and health and wellness.

ISOPROPYL ALCOHOL (RUBBING ALCOHOL)

Isopropyl alcohol, also called rubbing alcohol, is a clear liquid prepared from a denatured alcohol solution. It usually contains 70% by volume pure isopropyl alcohol. It is most widely used as a topical solution for disinfection and can also be used for household cleaning.

JOJOBA OIL

Jojoba oil comes from the seeds of the jojoba plant, *Simmondsia chinensis*. When the pure oil is extracted from the seeds, it is in liquid form and is gold in color. Jojoba oil's chemical makeup is very close to human sebum. It is antibacterial and is loaded with beneficial minerals and vitamins. It is commonly used in the cosmetic field as a makeup remover and body moisturizer and for conditioning treatments.

PURE SOAP FLAKES

Pure soap flakes are small, silky flakes made from concentrated castile soap, typically from 100% plant oils. Sodium hydroxide is mixed with these plant oils to create pure soap flakes. Soap flakes can be used to make laundry detergent, body and baby soap, and many other natural cleaning products.

SALT

Salt is a white crystalline substance that is commonly used in the kitchen to season and preserve foods. Salt can also be used to drive away ants and get rid of stains. It is also an effective antiseptic.

SHEA BUTTER

Shea butter is a vegetable fat that is ivory in color and silky in texture. It comes from the nuts of the African shea tree. It is used in the cosmetic industry and for many do-it-yourself recipes. Uses for shea butter range from homemade deodorants and creamy lotions to skin rash creams and eczema creams.

VEGETABLE GLYCERIN (FOOD GRADE)

Vegetable glycerin is made from plant oils, usually palm and coconut oils. It is an odorless, thick liquid that is used in many do-it-yourself cosmetic products. Vegetable glycerin helps emulsify ingredients. Make sure that the vegetable glycerin you get is food-grade quality. Common uses for vegetable glycerin include moisturizing, cleansing and acne relief.

VITAMIN E OIL

Vitamin E oil is an antioxidant with many beneficial healing properties. It can be used as a natural preservative that is perfect for homemade products. It is commonly used in the cosmetic industry and in do-it-yourself natural solutions for lotions, face washes and lip balms.

WASHING SODA

Washing soda is a natural cleaning product made of sodium carbonate. It softens hard water and foams freely, cleaning the toughest stains. Washing soda is great for laundry and cleaning bathroom tiles, and it makes a great dishwasher detergent.

WITCH HAZEL

Witch hazel is a North American shrub. Its bark and leaves are often used as medicine. Witch hazel extract and water are combined to create witch hazel water that is commonly found in drug stores. Common uses for witch hazel water are to help fade bruises, heal blemishes, relieve hemorrhoids, ease sore throats and repair damaged gums.

ZINC OXIDE POWDER & ZINC SULFATE

Zinc oxide powder is a topical powder that is commonly used for sunscreen, healing acne and healing skin problems. Zinc sulfate is a mineral that is typically used for getting rid of warts.

EQUIPMENT RECOMMENDED FOR NATURAL SOLUTIONS

Here is a list of suggested equipment handy for making natural solutions:

SPRAY BOTTLES

A variety of sizes works best. Look for fine mist sprayers and sprayers that can change from stream to spray.

SQUEEZE TOP BOTTLES

A variety of sizes are good to have on hand. These are incredibly handy for shampoos, face washes and dish soaps.

SHAKER BOTTLES

Shaker bottles are great for dry shampoos, scouring powders and air fresheners. You can use old Parmesan cheese containers and empty glass spice jars.

SPONGES

Sponges that have a soft surface on one side and a medium abrasive on the other make cleaning tough stains a lot easier.

NYLON SCRUBBING BRUSH

Nylon scrubbing brushes usually don't scratch the surface you are working on. They are much gentler than scouring pads, and they still get the job done.

OLD TOOTHBRUSH

Toothbrushes get into hard-to-reach areas and small areas that you want to clean.

MICROFIBER CLOTHS

Want streak-free cleaning? Try microfiber cloths. They are incredibly effective and you can use them over and over.

CONTAINERS

Multiple container sizes are helpful. Look to stock some 4-ounce (118-ml), 8-ounce (237-ml), 12-ounce (355-ml) and 16-ounce (473-ml) containers with lids.

FOAMING AND REGULAR SOAP DISPENSERS

Making liquid and foaming hand soap is super easy and will save you a lot of money. Pick up a few regular empty pump soap dispensers and a few foaming pump soap dispensers. You can also recycle used soap dispensers.

GALLON JUGS

Gallon jugs are great for liquid laundry detergent. Save an old distilled water jug or even a washed-out empty milk jug.

FLIP-TOP GLASS BOTTLES

Flip-top glass bottles are super convenient for storing shampoos and conditioners. They are great for soft scrubs and lotions, too.

HIGH-SPEED BLENDER

A high-speed blender is handy for emulsifying ingredients together. You can also use a stick blender (immersion blender).

OLD CANS OR JARS

When you're using waxes such as beeswax and carnauba wax, it is really hard to get them off of surfaces. Dedicate an old can or even a glass mason jar for preparing these solutions.

MASON JARS

Mason jars are great for storage and can be converted into hand soap jars.

MEASURING UTENSILS (CUPS, SPOONS)

Have a good supply of measuring cups and measuring spoons. You can also use a digital scale if that method is easier for you.

LARGE 3-GALLON (11.4-L) BUCKET

For cleaning large areas such as a grill or a car, a bigger bucket is needed.

Consider recycling old and previously used containers to store your homemade solutions.

PART ONE

NATURAL SOLUTIONS FOR THE HOME

BATHROOM

Cleaning a bathroom can be a dirty job. Many of the commercial products used today are full of chemicals and can be harmful to your health. With a couple of easy changes, you can quickly make your bathroom non-toxic.

Baking soda goes a long way in the bathroom. Use it to clean the toilets and scour the bathtub or shower. Baking soda can also be used to eliminate odor. We all know bathrooms can get stinky fast!

Hydrogen peroxide is another great ingredient for the bathroom. It disinfects surfaces and cleans windows like nothing else. It can clean tile and grout better than any commercial products.

Vinegar is the holy grail of natural cleaners! I use it in almost every chapter of this book. It is great for cleaning toilets, removing mold and mildew and breaking down soap scum. It easily gets rid of hard water buildup in a matter of minutes.

Essential oils can also be helpful for cleaning bathrooms. They provide antibacterial and anti-fungal protection. Some oils, especially lemon oil, help cut through grease and soap scum and can even help eliminate strong odors that are often present in bathrooms.

Gear yourself up with these ingredients and you will have your bathroom sparking in no time. The best part might be that your bathroom will have no traces of chemicals in it, so you'll be assured that you have a safe room where you can retreat.

TOILET CLEANER

Cleaning the toilet doesn't have to be a gross job. This solution creates its own fizzy bubbles, which clean the toilet for you. It's that easy!

Yield: 1 cup (237 ml)

¼ cup (52 g) baking soda

¾ cup (177 ml) distilled white vinegar

3% hydrogen peroxide

Sprinkle all of the baking soda into the toilet bowl and add the vinegar. This will create fizzy bubbles. Shut the lid and allow the bubbles to do their magic for 5 minutes. After 5 minutes, scrub the toilet bowl well. Flush.

For the outside of the toilet bowl, use undiluted hydrogen peroxide. Spray hydrogen peroxide onto the outside of the surface, including the seat and the base of the toilet, and wipe clean. You can also add a tablespoon (15 ml) of hydrogen peroxide to a small damp towel and wipe the surface clean.

EXTRA TIP...

Want to add a fresh smell to your bathroom after cleaning it? Check out page 72 to find four creative ways to keep your bathroom smelling fresh.

SOFT SCRUB BATHTUB, SHOWER AND SINK CLEANER

Sometimes you need a cleaner that can easily be made with a few quality ingredients and still has the incredible cleaning capabilities of a commercial cleaning product. This is that cleaner.

Yield: about 1½ cups (355 ml)

1 cup (206 g) baking soda

½ cup (118 ml) boiling water

2 tbsp (30 ml) lavender liquid castile soap (unscented liquid castile soap can also be used)

In a small bowl, add the baking soda. Pour the boiling water over the baking soda and mix with a wire whisk until the solution is dissolved and well blended, about 2 minutes. Whisk in the liquid castile soap. Pour the mixture into a squeezable container.

To clean the shower and/or bathtub, squeeze the soft scrub onto the surface or directly onto the sponge. Scrub and clean the surface. Rinse. If the soft scrub thickens as it sits, just add water to thin and shake gently to combine.

This soft scrub cleaner can also be used to clean sinks and toilets.

Baking soda is so universal when making natural solutions. It removes stains, eliminates odors and can safely be used as a natural fire extinguisher.

MOLD AND MILDEW CLEANER

Several formulas can help you get rid of mold and mildew. I am providing two. Both are effective, but do not use a vinegar or acidic base solution on any stone surface (such as granite). Vinegar can also break down grout over time, so use the vinegar solution sparingly if you have grout. Be sure to test these formulas on a small section of the surface to make sure they're safe for your particular surface.

Yield: 1 cup (237 ml) each

SOLUTION #1
1 cup (237 ml) 3% hydrogen peroxide

SOLUTION #2
1 cup (237 ml) distilled white vinegar

10 drops melaleuca (tea tree) oil

SOLUTION #1:
Pour the hydrogen peroxide into a spray bottle. Spray the entire surface from which you want to eliminate mold and mildew. Allow the solution to sit for 15 minutes and then rinse off.

SOLUTION #2
Pour the distilled white vinegar into a spray bottle. Add the melaleuca oil and shake well. Spray the solution onto the entire surface and allow to dry fully. Do not rinse. This method has a strong odor, but the odor will dissipate after a few hours.

DID YOU KNOW...

Mold and mildew can cause allergies. Maleleuca, also known as tea tree oil, is an antibacterial, antifungal and anti-infectious essential oil. Maleleuca is also beneficial for allergy relief.

SOAP SCUM CLEANER

Soap scum can be very difficult to remove. Here is a way to get rid of it once and for all! For tougher soap scum buildup, you may need to repeat this procedure several times.

Yield: about 2 ¾ cups (650 ml)

1½ cups (355 ml) warm distilled water (not regular tap water)

2 tsp (10 g) kosher salt

¾ cup (177 ml) Dr. Bronner's Sal Suds (not castile soap)

½ cup (118 ml) distilled white vinegar

Lemon essential oil (optional)

In a medium bowl, add the warm distilled water and dissolve the kosher salt. Do not leave out the salt: it thickens the solution. Stir in the Sal Suds and the distilled white vinegar. Pour into a spray bottle.

Turn on the shower as hot as it will go and run it for 5 minutes. The steam from the shower will help loosen the soap scum.

Liberally spray this solution directly onto the soap scum. Let sit for 15 minutes. For tough soap scum, allow the solution to sit for up to an hour. Completely rinse off the solution and watch the soap scum disappear.

For glass surfaces, once your soap scum is completely removed, add a few drops of lemon oil to a cloth and wipe it on the glass. This will help prevent future soap scum buildup.

As a daily shower routine to prevent any further soap scum, squeegee the shower dry or dry it completely with a towel.

A combination of vinegar and Dr. Bronner's Sal Suds safely cleans and eliminates soap scum. To prevent soap scum from coming back, always rinse and dry your surface after each use.

SCOURING POWDER

Sometimes you need a strong scouring powder that can get just about anything clean. These three ingredients mixed together creates one of the best scouring powders available.

Yield: 1 cup (180 g)

½ cup (90 g) diatomaceous earth

½ cup (103 g) baking soda

6-8 drops lemon essential oil (optional)

Mix together the diatomaceous earth and baking soda and stir well. Add 6-8 drops of lemon essential oil if desired and shake well.

Transfer to a shaker bottle (I like to reuse glass spice jars), and shake a small amount onto the surface that needs cleaning. Scour the surface with a sponge, adding a little water if needed until surface comes clean.

This scouring powder is useful for toilets, bathtubs, showers, stainless steel and glass surfaces. Avoid using this on stone surfaces and copper.

DID YOU KNOW...

Diatomaceous earth is a hidden secret. It is extremely affordable and has so many uses. It is most commonly used as an insecticide. Diatomaceous earth can get rid of ants, fleas, bed bugs and roaches without the use of any chemicals.

GROUT CLEANER

Cleaning grout can be quite a challenge. My two solutions are incredibly effective. Both solutions require a little scrubbing, but the results are well worth it. When cleaning grout, always use a heavy-duty nylon brush.

Yield: varies

SOLUTION 1:

3% hydrogen peroxide

Baking soda

SOLUTION 2:

Distilled white vinegar

SOLUTION #1

If you have colored grout, be sure to test this solution in a small spot before cleaning all of it.

Liberally pour hydrogen peroxide on the grout and generously sprinkle baking soda on top of it. Let sit for 15 minutes.

After 15 minutes, scrub the grout solution with a nylon brush. Finish with a final rinse.

SOLUTION #2

Put vinegar into a spray bottle and spray the grout. Let sit for 5 minutes. With a nylon brush, scrub the grout clean. Finish with a rinse.

Vinegar can be harsh on grout, so be sure to use this method sparingly.

HARD WATER DEPOSIT REMOVER

Hard water deposits can be nasty to look at and even nastier to clean. These deposits can show up in the shower or even in the kitchen on items such as ice and water trays. Here is a simple solution that will allow you to wipe away those deposits.

Yield: 1¼ cups (225 ml)

1 cup (237 ml) distilled white vinegar

¼ cup (60 ml) lemon juice

Combine the vinegar and lemon juice in a bowl. If the item is removable (such as an ice or water tray), remove it and place it in a bucket. Cover the item with the vinegar and lemon solution and allow it to soak for 5 minutes, or longer for really thick buildup. After it has soaked, scrub with a nylon brush until it comes clean. Deposits will come right off.

If the hard water deposit is on a showerhead, soak a towel (large enough to cover the shower head) in a bucket of the vinegar and lemon juice solution. Take the towel and wrap it around the showerhead and secure it with a rubber band. Place a plastic bag over the towel and allow it to sit for 5 minutes, or longer for really thick buildup. Remove the towel and bag and wipe the hard water deposits off with a clean towel.

Lemon juice and vinegar create an acidic solution that easily dissolves excess hard water buildup.

EXTRA TIP…

To prevent hard water buildup in the future, dry the surface with a towel after each use. This will prevent the water from evaporating, which leaves hard water spots.

MIRROR CLEANER

Cleaning a mirror isn't hard, but getting it streak-free does require a few key techniques.

Yield: 1½ cups (355 ml)

1 cup (237 ml) water

½ cup (118 ml) distilled white vinegar

Rubbing alcohol

Cotton pad

Microfiber cloth or newspaper

In a spray bottle, mix together the water and vinegar. Place a little rubbing alcohol on a cotton pad and remove any dirt, smudges, toothpaste or anything else that might be on the mirror. Be sure to do this before you use the water and vinegar mix.

Spray the mirror with the vinegar and water mixture. With a microfiber cloth, start at the top of the mirror and wipe from left to right, working your way all the way down the mirror.

If you do not have a microfiber cloth, use an old newspaper.

EXTRA TIP...

If the mirror has a light over it, turn the light off while you are cleaning it. The heat from the lightbulb can dry the surface too quickly and will create unwanted streaks. Once you've finished cleaning, turn the light back on to view your streak-free mirror.

KITCHEN

If there was ever a room to clean naturally, it would have to be the kitchen. So much of our food touches the surfaces of the kitchen. If you are using chemicals to clean your kitchen, you are most likely absorbing some of the chemicals in the cleaners.

Many people think that strong cleaning supplies are needed to prevent food-borne illnesses. This is not true. You can completely clean your kitchen with natural ingredients by following simple steps to keep bacteria and viruses away from food—and more importantly, away from you!

Some common ingredients used to clean the kitchen are vinegar and baking soda, but some simple food items can help as well.

We often use salt to season our food. Did you know that it can also help clean a cast iron skillet? It's true! It removes all those dried-on, stubborn tidbits in no time. Salt also helps thicken certain soaps. My lemon dish soap has salt in it for this very reason. Salt also helps soften water, which helps your dishes get cleaner.

Lemon is another good kitchen-cleaning ingredient. Lemon helps cut through grease and can get a microwave oven clean in a matter of minutes. It can also be used to clean cutting boards or other wood surfaces, and it is the single best ingredient for cleaning solid copper.

It doesn't take much to transform your kitchen into a natural kitchen. Follow these solutions, practice safe handling procedures and always wash your produce before eating. Wipe up immediately and clean your refrigerator often. With these simple steps, you will be on your way to a safe and clean kitchen.

LEMON DISH SOAP

When making homemade dish soap, you want suds! This solution has suds, cuts through grease and softens your hands. It is important to note that it is best not to use essential oils in this recipe, as they can alter the effectiveness. Plus, it already has a great natural pine and lemon scent.

Yield: about 3¼ cups (770 ml)

2 cups (473 ml) filtered water

1 tbsp (15 g) + 1 tsp (5 g) kosher salt

1 cup (237 ml) Dr. Bronner's Sal Suds

1 whole lemon, juiced

2 tbsp (28 g) pure aloe vera

In a large bowl, warm up the filtered water. Add the salt and stir until it is fully dissolved. Next, add in the Sal Suds, lemon juice and aloe vera and stir until well blended. The dish soap will thicken immediately. Pour into an old dish soap container and use as you would any dish soap.

DID YOU KNOW…

Lemon juice helps disinfect and also acts as a natural degreaser.

Pure aloe vera is an incredible hand moisturizer in this dish soap.

When using liquid castile soap or Dr. Bonner's Sal Suds, you can easily thicken certain solutions by adding a bit of kosher salt.

POWDERED DISHWASHER DETERGENT AND RINSE AID

No more expensive products; this one will cost you only pennies per load! It can be hard to create an all-natural dishwasher solution that actually works. After many attempts, I found it crucial to add a few drops of dish soap. Please do not leave it out, but use ONLY three drops. If you do leave it out, your dishes will still come clean, but the glassware and plastic might end up with a cloudy film.

Yield: 1¼ cups (225 g) powdered dishwasher detergent, 1½ cups (118 ml) rinse aide

1 cup (206 g) washing soda

¼ cup (60 g) kosher salt

3 drops Lemon Dish Soap (page 34)

½ cup (118 ml) distilled white vinegar

Mix together the washing soda and kosher salt. Store in an airtight container.

For each load, add 1 tablespoon (13 g) of the mixture and 3 drops of Lemon Dish Soap (no more) to the detergent compartment. Add the vinegar to the bottom of the dishwasher and wash as usual.

Washing soda safely and effectively cleans dishes, clothes and eliminates stubborn odors found in sponges.

ALL-PURPOSE DISINFECTANT CLEANER

You may think that an all-natural disinfectant requires a complicated recipe with complicated ingredients. The truth is that you need only two or three ingredients for an incredibly effective disinfectant.

Yield: 2 cups (474 ml)

1 cup (237 ml) water

1 cup (237 ml) hydrogen peroxide

Essential oils (optional)

Add all the ingredients to a dark spray bottle. It is important that hydrogen peroxide stay in a dark container so that it does not lose its effectiveness. Shake the solution, spray on the surface and wipe clean.

A few essential oils that help with disinfection are melaleuca, lemon and eucalyptus. Do not use lemon on stone surfaces, such as granite.

DID YOU KNOW...

Hydrogen peroxide kills bacteria, mold, mildew and fungus. Hydrogen peroxide also dries streak-free, making it a perfect cleaner for mirrors and windows. If you buy a 32-ounce (946-ml) bottle of hydrogen peroxide, you can replace the lid with a spray nozzle so you don't have to worry about buying a dark spray bottle.

STAINLESS STEEL CLEANER

Have you ever used olive oil to clean your stainless steel? I struggled with this method because olive oil does nothing to disinfect the surface, and over time it can leave a buildup on the stainless steel. Using hydrogen peroxide to clean stainless steel will disinfect the surface and leave it streak-free. A win-win!

Yield: varies

70% isopropyl rubbing alcohol

3% food-grade hydrogen peroxide

Microfiber cloth

When cleaning stainless steel, always clean with the grain of the steel to avoid scratching the surface. It is best to use a soft microfiber cloth to clean and polish your stainless steel.

Put a little rubbing alcohol onto a cotton pad and gently rub off any surface dirt. Be sure to remove all food particles and grease spots before wiping with hydrogen peroxide.

After spot cleaning, spray some hydrogen peroxide onto the surface and let it sit for about a minute. It is best to use a fine mist spray bottle so that the solution doesn't run off.

Wipe off the solution by starting at the top of the surface and moving downward and in a left-to-right motion. Always follow the grain of the stainless steel when cleaning it. This will prevent scratching or damaging the surface.

Finish with a microfiber cloth, starting from the top and moving downward, from left to right. This final step with help polish the surface and ensure that there are no streaks.

GRANITE COUNTERTOP CLEANER

Granite is a popular countertop surface in kitchens today. It is a great surface because it is hard and heat-resistant as well as easy to maintain. Here is a solution that will safely clean and disinfect stone.

Yield: 3⅓ cups (788 ml)

Warm water

⅓ cup (78 ml) 70% rubbing alcohol

3 cups (710 ml) distilled water

Wipe the entire surface clean with warm water. Allow to dry. Pour the rubbing alcohol and the distilled water into a spray bottle and shake.

Spray the solution onto the granite and wipe clean with a paper towel. This single process safely disinfects the counters and cleans them, too.

DID YOU KNOW...

You should never use anything acidic on solid stone surfaces such as granite. Avoid ammonia, vinegar and citrus (including citrus essential oils). These acids can leave scratches.

Alcohol is a natural disinfectant. It also dries quickly, which helps prevent streaks.

DEGREASER

Sometimes you need more than hot water to clean up a stain. Grease can be incredibly stubborn to clean, so it requires a few more ingredients. This solution works well on stovetops. For bigger jobs, such as the entire oven, check out the Oven Cleaner solution on page 41.

Yield: 2³/₄ cups (650 ml)

1½ cups (355 ml) warm distilled water

2 tsp (10 g) kosher salt

¾ cup (177 ml) Dr. Bronner's Sal Suds

½ cup (118 ml) distilled white vinegar

Add the warm distilled water to a medium-sized bowl and dissolve the kosher salt. Do not leave the salt out of this solution, as this thickens the degreaser. Add the Sal Suds and vinegar and stir lightly. Pour into a spray bottle. To use, spray directly on grease. A little of this solution goes a long way, so don't overspray. Wipe clean with a warm, damp sponge.

SAFETY NOTE...

Do not mistake castile soap for Dr. Bronner's Sal Suds. They are two completely different cleaning agents and cannot be substituted for one another.

ELIMINATE SPONGE ODOR

It seems like every few days you have to replace a sponge because it smells. Bacteria can quickly grow on sponges, so it is important to clean them regularly with a simple solution. You can dramatically extend the life of your sponge by following these simple steps.

Yield: about 1 cup (237 ml)

---

1 cup (237 ml) warm water

1 tbsp (13 g) washing soda

Add the warm water and washing soda to a medium-sized bowl. Stir to dissolve. Place the sponge into the solution and let soak for a few hours. Remove the sponge and squeeze out any remaining water. Allow to dry fully before using. Repeat this once a week to keep your sponges smelling fresh.

MICROWAVE OVEN CLEANER

One of the most effective ways to clean a microwave is to use it while cleaning it. Creating enough steam and humidity is the key to cleaning a microwave! Doing this will allow you to wipe up the grease and food particles with one simple swipe of the cloth.

Yield: about 3½ cups (830 ml)

1 lemon

3 cups (710 ml) water

Cut the lemon in half and place it in a large bowl. Pour the water over the lemon halves.

Microwave on high until the water boils, for about 3 minutes for most microwaves. When the 3 minutes are up, leave the door shut for another 10 minutes so the steam can loosen any debris. Open the door and wipe the surface clean.

Lemons are often used on hard to clean and stubborn surfaces. The acid in the lemon juice cuts through grease incredibly well.

DID YOU KNOW...

Lemon is a natural degreaser. Lemon juice can also be used to reduce oily skin. Place some lemon juice on a cotton pad and gently wipe your face before bed. In no time, your skin will become less oily. Lemon juice can also be used as a natural body cleanser. Add it to your favorite body wash (or see page 138) and enjoy an extra cleaning boost that refreshes and cleans like nothing else.

OVEN CLEANER

Oven cleaners on the market today are some of the most toxic products out there. With a few ingredients and very little elbow grease, you can have your oven sparkling in no time!

Yield: varies

½ cup (103 g) baking soda

¼ cup (60 ml) water

Distilled white vinegar

3% food-grade hydrogen peroxide

In a small bowl, combine the baking soda and water to form a thick paste. Spread over the entire oven, including the glass door, if any. Let it sit for 5 minutes.

Pour some distilled white vinegar into a spray bottle. Spray the entire surface that is covered with the baking soda paste. It will foam up slightly. Let the bubble reaction work for 5 more minutes.

With warm water and a sponge, wipe the surface area clean, scrubbing where needed.

Finish by spraying the glass door with hydrogen peroxide and wipe from left to right, drying the glass completely to create a streak-free door.

GARBAGE DISPOSAL CLEANER

Bacteria can grow quickly in a garbage disposal, so it is important to clean it about every two weeks. It doesn't take long to clean a disposal, and it will run more smoothly if you do.

Yield: varies

½ cup (120 g) rock salt

1 cup (a large handful) ice cubes

½ cup (103 g) baking soda

1 cup (237 ml) distilled white vinegar

Lemon or orange peels (optional)

Pour the rock salt down the drain and add the ice. Run the disposal for about 2 minutes. This will get all the grime and food particles off of the grind ring.

With the disposal off and unplugged, pour the baking soda and vinegar down the drain. Let it fizz for about 15 minutes. After 15 minutes, run hot water down the drain and turn on the disposal for about 1 minute.

If you desire a fresh citrus scent, finish by putting some lemon or orange peels down the drain and run the disposal for 30 more seconds.

DRAIN CLOG REMOVER

Clogged drains can be problematic if they are not dealt with right away. Before you call the plumber, try this effective method for cleaning and clearing a clogged drain.

Yield: varies

½ cup (103 g) baking soda

1 cup (237 ml) distilled white vinegar

4 cups (947 ml) hot water

Pour the baking soda down the drain and then add the vinegar. This creates a fizzy and foaming action that will help break down the clog in the drain. Let this solution sit in the drain for 20 minutes.

Flush out the drain by pouring very hot (but not boiling) water down the drain. If it is still clogged, try using a plunger with another 4 cups (947 ml) of very hot water. Repeat if necessary.

SAFETY NOTES...

If anything electric is connected to the drain (such as a garbage disposal), unplug the item before you begin to work on it.

Do not use this solution if you have recently used a commercial product to unclog your drains. The baking soda and vinegar could react with the commercial product's ingredients, creating fumes that might be dangerous.

COFFEE POT AND
COFFEE MACHINE CLEANER

Getting rid of tough buildup in coffee machines can be a challenge. Not only does this buildup look bad, but it can change the flavor profile of your coffee, making it taste stale and somewhat "off." Here is a simple solution that will clean your coffee pot and machine.

Yield: coffee pot: about 1¼ cups (300 ml), coffee machine: about 12 cups (3 L)

FOR COFFEE POT

1 cup (a large handful) ice

2 tbsp (30 g) kosher salt

1 tbsp (15 ml) distilled white vinegar

FOR COFFEE MACHINE

4 cups (947 ml) distilled white vinegar

8–12 cups (1.8–2.8 L) water

In a room temperature coffee pot, add ice, kosher salt and distilled vinegar. Swish the ice around for several minutes. This will clean the pot, and the acidic vinegar will break down the stains. For really stubborn stains, let the solution sit in the pot for 5 minutes. Pour out the solution and wash in cold water. Stains will wipe right off.

If the outside of the coffee machine is dirty, use vinegar to wipe it clean. To clean the inside, run distilled white vinegar through a cycle. Be sure to put in an empty coffee filter. After this cycle, dispose of the vinegar and run the water through a cycle. Discard and run one more cycle of 8–12 cups (1.8–2.8 L) of water. The machine is now clean and ready for your next brew.

For best results, clean your coffee machine with this method once a month.

CAST IRON SKILLET CLEANER

Cast iron skillets are some of the easiest to cook on when they're properly seasoned. Once they're seasoned, you should never use soap or cleaners on them. Here is how to properly clean a cast iron skillet.

Yield: varies

Hot water

1–3 tbsp (15–45 g) kosher salt

1–2 tsp (5–10 ml) olive oil

Put some hot water into the skillet. With a sponge or a stiff brush, scrub the skillet clean. If there is a lot of caked-on food, generously sprinkle with kosher salt. (Kosher salt is a soft, flaky salt that will not damage your skillet.) Rub the kosher salt into the skillet with a circular motion, and the food particles will come right off. Rinse the skillet in clean, hot water and rub olive oil over the entire surface, including the outside of the skillet.

DID YOU KNOW...

To prevent rust from forming on a cast iron skillet, you need to oil your pan after each use, right after cleaning.

Do not clean your cast iron skillet with soap. Salt effectively cleans a seasoned cast iron skillet followed with a quick rinse of water.

SILVER AND TARNISH CLEANER

Silver can tarnish quickly. There are a ton of recipes out there for homemade cleaners, but many of them will actually damage your silver. Here is a solution that will not damage your silver. It might take a bit more elbow grease and time than some others, but rest assured that your fine silver will not be damaged by harsh chemicals or cleaning techniques.

Yield: about 3 tbsp (48 g)

¼ cup (45 g) calcium carbonate powder

Distilled water

Make a fluffy paste out of the calcium carbonate by adding distilled water. You don't want this paste to be too runny or too thick; look for the consistency of a lighter foam.

With a cotton pad, rub the mixture onto the silver and let it sit for a few minutes. Use a toothbrush to get into tight grooves and smaller spaces. With a cotton pad, rub the mixture off of the silver in a circular motion until the tarnish disappears. If there is a lot of tarnish on an object, a second application might be needed.

Once the tarnish has been removed, rinse with distilled water and dry. Finish by polishing with a silver polishing cloth.

SOLID COPPER CLEANER

There are a few things to consider when cleaning copper. For instance, is your item solid copper or is it only plated with copper? This makes a difference because you can damage plated copper with certain cleaning methods. To find out whether your item is copper or not, place a magnet on it. If it sticks, it is plated copper. If the magnet does not stick, then your item is solid copper.

If you have plated copper, clean it only with warm soapy water and a soft cloth, and dry it.

Yield: varies

¼ cup (60 g. plus more if needed) table salt (do not use coarse salt)

1 lemon

Always test your copper to see if you have solid copper or plated copper. Both have different cleaning methods so it is important to know which kind of copper you have.

Place the table salt in a shallow bowl. Cut the lemon in half and dip it into the salt. Generously rub a thick layer of the lemon and salt all over the copper and wait for 20 seconds. With a sponge, begin removing the tarnish by gently rubbing in a circular motion. Repeat as needed until all of the tarnish is gone. Completely rinse the item with warm water and dry it with a soft cloth.

If you are worried about the salt scratching the surface of a particular piece, squeeze some lemon juice into a bowl and add the salt to make a paste. Let it sit for a few minutes so that the salt dissolves a little and makes a less coarse solution.

EXTRA TIP...

Another consideration is whether your copper has a lacquered top layer. Lacquer has a shiny appearance similar to that of clear nail polish. If you have lacquered copper, do not use this cleaning method—use only warm water with a mild dish soap. If the lacquer is scratched or damaged and the copper underneath is tarnishing, you may want to consider removing the lacquer. To remove the lacquer, place 2 quarts (1.9 L) of water in a large saucepan and bring it to a boil. Dissolve ½ cup (103 g) baking soda in the boiling water. Carefully add your piece to the solution. The lacquer should peel right off. A scum-like substance could float to the surface. Remove your item from the solution and polish off any remaining lacquer. Repeat if needed.

CUTTING BOARD CLEANER

It is important to clean your cutting boards on a regular basis. Certain bacteria and viruses can grow on these surfaces, potentially causing someone to get really sick. Follow these simple steps to clean and disinfect your wooden and plastic cutting boards.

Yield: varies

Soapy hot water

2 tbsp (30 g) kosher salt

1 lemon

3% food-grade hydrogen peroxide

Wash the cutting board with soapy hot water. Let dry. Meanwhile, place the kosher salt in a shallow bowl. Cut the lemon in half and dip the lemon into the salt. Generously rub a thick layer of the lemon and salt solution all over the cutting board and scour into the grain of the board. Leave the solution on for 5 minutes.

With a bench scraper, scrape the surface, removing the grit. Repeat as needed until the board is clean. Completely rinse the cutting board with warm water and dry. Finish by spraying food-grade hydrogen peroxide on the board. Let it sit for 5 minutes and rinse once more with warm water.

After each use, clean with soapy hot water. Always disinfect with food-grade 3% hydrogen peroxide. For maintenance, follow the lemon and salt method a few times a month, or more for heavy use.

LAUNDRY

Have you ever noticed how expensive common laundry supplies are? Laundry detergent alone can run you close to $20. Ouch!

It doesn't have to cost a lot of money to do your laundry. All you need is a few natural ingredients that, surprisingly, are very inexpensive. They will transform your laundry experience.

Vinegar is the most treasured ingredient in my laundry room. It cuts through stains, eliminates odor and softens clothes like nothing else. If the smell of vinegar is a bit strong for you, you can add in some essential oils to help offset the odor. I've found that the more I use vinegar, the more I get used to the sour but pleasant scent.

Another ingredient I use in the laundry room is Dr. Bronner's Sal Suds. This is an incredible spot remover, and it makes some of the best liquid laundry detergent that I have ever used. Washing soda is great for powdered laundry detergent. It makes incredible suds and it fights to get grimy and dingy clothes clean.

Baking soda is also a must in the laundry room. It starts to eliminate odor on contact. One of the top complaints I hear from people is that their towels smell sour. This sour smell is usually caused by a buildup of soap, fabric softener or both. To strip those ingredients out of the towels, simply use baking soda. It works like a charm, and in no time you will have clean-smelling towels once again.

With a small handful of natural ingredients, you can successfully disinfect, clean and eliminate odors for all your laundry needs. Best of all, you can save a lot of money in the process! A win–win for sure.

POWDER LAUNDRY DETERGENT

One of the quickest ways to save money in the home is to make your own laundry detergent. It takes just minutes, and the ingredients are reasonably priced.

Yield: 3 cups (540 g)

½ cup (103 g) baking soda

1 cup (203 g) washing soda

1 cup (203 g) borax

½ cup (38 g) pure soap flakes

20 drops lemon essential oil (optional)

Mix together all the ingredients and store in a dry container.

For high-efficiency washing machines, use 1 tablespoon (13 g) per load. Pour directly over clothes. If using hot water, there is no need to dissolve. If using warm or cold water, dissolve 1 tablespoon (13 g) of detergent with 1 cup (237 ml) of very hot water and fully dissolve before adding it to the laundry.

Use ¼–½ cup (51–103 g) per load for non-high-efficiency washing machines. Dissolve in 2 cups (473 ml) hot water if washing in warm or cold water.

Store-bought laundry detergent can be pricey! You can easily make your own laundry detergent for a fraction of the cost with only a few quality ingredients.

EXTRA TIP...

Did you forget some laundry in the washing machine overnight? Add a few drops of lemon oil to a rinse cycle and it will no longer smell.

LIQUID LAUNDRY DETERGENT

Some people prefer liquid detergent over powder detergent. Being already fully dissolved, it's super convenient. It is best to not use any essential oils in this laundry detergent because they might affect the thickness of the detergent. If you want to use essential oils, add them in the rinse cycle.

Yield: 8½ cups (2 L)

6 cups (1.4 L) warm distilled water

4 tbsp (60 g) kosher salt

2¼ cups (405 g) Dr. Bronner's Sal Suds

In a large container, mix the warm distilled water with the salt and stir to dissolve. The salt thickens the soap, so do not leave it out. Stir in the Sal Suds. Pour the detergent into a large container. Use ¼ cup (52 g) detergent per load for high efficiency and ½ cup (60 ml) liquid detergent per load for standard washing machines.

LEMON BLEACH ALTERNATIVE

Who knew that a common kitchen ingredient is also beneficial in the laundry room? Did you know that lemon juice and the sun can bring your grimy whites back to a bright and vibrant white? I would not use this on colored garments because it could leave bleach marks. Also, do not use this solution on delicate fabrics such as silk.

Yield: 1 gallon + ½ cup (4 L)

½ cup (118 ml) lemon juice

1 gallon (4 L) hot water

Mix the lemon juice into the gallon of hot water. For extremely dingy white clothing, soak in the solution for an hour or longer. For less dingy whites, simply add ½ cup (118 ml) lemon juice to the wash cycle. Wash as usual but do not tumble dry.

Hang the white articles in the sun for 2–3 hours to dry. The sun will add extra whitening power and should restore the whites back to their natural color.

SCENTED FABRIC SOFTENER

Did you know that vinegar is really the only ingredient that you need to soften your clothes? It also helps clean and disinfect them.

Yield: 1 quart (947 ml)

1 quart (947 ml) distilled white vinegar

25 drops essential oil (optional)

Vinegar softens clothes naturally. Add some dried or fresh herbs to the vinegar and let it sit for several weeks then strain your vinegar for a fresh-scented fabric softener.

Remove the lid from the vinegar and add 25 drops of your essential oil of choice. Shake well.

For high-efficiency washing machines, add ½ cup (118 ml) to the rinse cycle dispenser and proceed as usual. For standard washing machines, add 1 cup (237 ml) to the rinse cycle.

HERE ARE SOME OIL SUGGESTIONS THAT WORK REALLY WELL WITH LAUNDRY

Spring (fresh-smelling scents)—lemon, lavender, cilantro

Summer (citrus scents)—wild orange, grapefruit, lime, lemon

Fall (warming, spicy scents)—lavender, juniper berry, cinnamon, nutmeg

Winter (uplifting oils to help with the winter blues)—peppermint, wintergreen, lavender, orange

WASHING MACHINE DEODORIZER

High-efficiency washing machines are very popular today. Unfortunately, there seems to be a common complaint: they can smell!

There are several reasons a washing machine might begin to smell. You might be using too much detergent. People often think that more is better when it comes to detergent, but this couldn't be further from the truth. On average, you should use only 1 tablespoon (15 ml) of concentrated detergent per load and 1/4 cup (60 ml) for non-concentrated detergent.

It could also be possible that you have mold growing in your washing machine. To check for it, open the machine door and look for a rubber piece surrounding the entire opening. Open it up. If you see brown or black spots trapped in between the rubber, you most likely have mold in your washing machine. Get a good nylon scrubbing brush and some vinegar and clean the entire surface.

Once you know where the odor is coming from, you want to maintain a clean washing machine. To do that, run vinegar through the rinse cycle of every load. Don't worry; your clothes will not smell like vinegar. If you'd prefer, you can do this once a week, but if the smell comes back, increase the frequency.

Yield: 1/2 cup (118 ml)

½–1 cup (118–237 ml) distilled white vinegar

In the rinse cycle compartment of your washing machine, add ½ cup (118 ml) of vinegar per load. Not only does it kill the odor, but it helps with cleaning and softening your clothes.

EXTRA TIP...

It is vital to leave the door of your front or top loader open after each use. If you close it, the moisture can stay in the unit, creating a perfect atmosphere for mold to grow. After each use, keep the door open and wipe the entire washer dry from any water. Be sure to pull back rubber pieces where water can get trapped.

SOUR TOWEL RELIEF

Have you ever gotten out of the shower and grabbed a clean towel only to find it has an unpleasant smell? Who wants to put that on their clean body? Sour towels are unpleasant, and there are often several reasons they begin to smell.

We often think more is better when it comes to detergent, but it isn't, especially with high-efficiency machines. On average you should use only 1 tablespoon (15 ml) of concentrated detergent per load and ¼ cup (60 ml) for non-concentrated detergent. Not a lot at all! A buildup of detergent can quickly turn into a sour smell. Resist using too much detergent.

Another problem is too much fabric softener. I find it best to use no fabric softener at all. If you want to soften your towels naturally, just add some vinegar to the final rinse cycle (page 53).

You can get clean towels once again by following some simple steps. The key is to get all the excess fabric softener and detergent out of the towels. You may have to follow these steps several times to achieve the desired results, but in time your towels will begin to smell pleasant again.

Yield: ½–1 cup (118–237 ml)

½–1 cup (103–203 g) baking soda

Add ½ cup (103 g) baking soda right on top of your towels if you have a high-efficiency top or front loader. If you have a standard washing machine, add 1 cup (203 g) of baking soda per load.

Don't add any detergent of any kind. Do not add fabric softener either.

The baking soda will begin to clean all the excess detergent and fabric softener out of the towels.

For the final step, hang your towels out in the sun. The UV rays will help disinfect and clean your towels naturally.

Towels often smell when one uses too much soap or fabric softener in their wash. If you are experiencing smelly towels, consider reducing or eliminating the soap and fabric softener from your wash.

BLOOD STAIN REMOVER

Blood really isn't that hard to remove from fabric if you have the proper ingredient. If you have it, blood stains will lift right out of your clothes before your eyes. This method works best as soon as you notice a blood stain. Test in a small spot to make sure it is safe for your particular fabric.

Yield: varies

3% hydrogen peroxide

Pour hydrogen peroxide right on the blood stain. The stain will fizz up and the blood will begin to break down. Leave on for 1 minute. With a toothbrush or nylon brush, rub the blood stain right out of the clothes. Wash immediately in a hot water cycle. Repeat if necessary.

LAUNDRY STAIN REMOVER

Creating a great stain remover only takes a few quality ingredients. This solution is incredibly effective and will take out just about any stain. Its semi-gel consistency helps it to stick to stains. For best results, treat stains as soon as you can and wash immediately.

Yield: 2 ¾ cups (650 ml)

1½ cups (355 ml) warm distilled water

2 tsp (10 g) kosher salt

¾ cup (155 g) Dr. Bronner's Sal Suds

½ cup (118 ml) vinegar

In a medium bowl, add the warm distilled water and dissolve the kosher salt. Do not leave the salt out of this solution; it thickens the stain remover. Add the Dr. Bonner's Sal Suds and vinegar and stir lightly. Pour into a spray bottle. To use, spray directly on stains. For tough stains, allow the solution to sit on the stain for 5–10 minutes before it goes in the wash.

EXTRA TIP…

This laundry stain remover can thicken as it sits. If the solution becomes too thick, a little water can be added to thin it out.

HOUSEHOLD CLEANING

What about natural solutions for cleaning rooms beyond the kitchen, bathroom and laundry room? You spend most of your time in those other rooms, so it is very important to eliminate toxic chemicals there, too.

I would like to highlight a few ingredients in this chapter. One is food-grade 3% hydrogen peroxide. Not only is hydrogen peroxide an excellent disinfectant, but it also cleans windows well and leaves them streak-free. Another great use for hydrogen peroxide is removing stains from furniture and carpets.

Liquid castile soap is also a useful general cleaner. It too can easily remove stains, help clean floors and make a foaming carpet stain remover to get out just about any stain.

Vodka is a surprisingly effective cleaner. It keeps bacteria from growing and helps eliminate the strongest of odors.

Lemon oil is one of the single best oils for household cleaning. It can remove crayon and pencil marks from walls, bring the shine and luster back to leather and help eliminate strong odors such as cigarette smoke.

Switching out commercial cleaners with a few quality natural ingredients can transform your well-being. It is worth your time and effort, and the rewards are huge: good health and longevity.

STREAK-FREE WINDOW CLEANER (INDOOR AND OUTDOOR)

Cleaning a window seems to be an easy task, but there are a few key rules to follow for getting a streak-free window.

Yield: indoor windows: 3 cups (710 ml), outdoor windows: 1 gallon (4 L)

INDOOR WINDOWS

2 cups (473 ml) warm water

1 cup (237 ml) 3% food-grade hydrogen peroxide

Rubbing alcohol

Microfiber cloth or newspaper

OUTDOOR WINDOWS

1 gallon (4 L) hot water

A few squirts of Lemon Dish Soap (page 34)

The key to getting streak-free windows is to remove the dirt, smudges and fingerprints with a little rubbing alcohol first.

FOR INDOOR WINDOWS

In a spray bottle, mix together the water and hydrogen peroxide. Place a little rubbing alcohol on a cotton pad and remove dirt, smudges, fingerprints and anything else that might be on the window. Be sure to do this before you use the hydrogen peroxide and water mixture.

Spray the window with the mixture. With a microfiber cloth, start at the top of the window and wipe from left to right, working all the way to the bottom. If you do not have a microfiber cloth, use an old newspaper.

FOR OUTDOOR WINDOWS

Use a squeegee for bigger jobs and outdoor windows. Try to find a squeegee that has a scrubbing bar on one side. Dip the scrubbing bar in the hot water and soap solution, or wet the scrubbing bar with hot water and add a little dish soap directly to the scrubber. Wash the windows with the soapy mixture. With the squeegee side, start at the top and work your way down the window in an "S" stroke. Dry your squeegee after each stroke with a lint-free towel or microfiber cloth.

For stubborn stains, or to get paint chips and other outdoor elements off the window, use a razor blade to gently scrape them. Test a small spot of the window first to make sure you won't scratch it.

GENERAL FLOOR CLEANER

This is a great all-purpose cleaner specifically designed for tile and solid surface flooring. It should not to be used on wood floors; try the Wood Floor Cleaner on page 60 instead. When using hydrogen peroxide, it is important always to test the surface with the solution to make sure it isn't damaging to that particular material.

Yield: 1 gallon + 1 cup (4 L)

1 gallon (4 L) warm water

1 cup (237 ml) 3% hydrogen peroxide

Mix together the warm water and hydrogen peroxide. Before mopping, it is always a good idea to vacuum or sweep up any dirt or dust. Once you have thoroughly cleaned the floors, generously soak a mop in the solution and wring it out. Scrub the floors clean and dry them completely before walking on them.

It is important to sweep before you mop the floors. The dirt and debris can scratch your floors during mopping so don't miss this critical step for clean floors.

WOOD FLOOR CLEANER

Always vacuum your wood floors before mopping them because the dirt and dust could scratch the floors when you mop. Turn off the roller brushes of your vacuum cleaner so you do not scratch the floors while vacuuming. Do not soak your wood floors. Use a damp mop only; do not use a dripping wet mop.

Yield: about 1 gallon (4 L)

1 gallon (4 L) warm water (do not use hot water; the heat might damage your floor)

2 tbsp (30 ml) liquid castile soap

Fill a large bucket with warm water. Add castile soap and stir. Dip a mop into the solution and squeeze out as much water as possible. Wash the wood floors by running the mop with the grain of the wood; do not go against the grain. Allow the floors to dry fully. If you want extra shine, gently buff your floors with a dry polish cloth.

EXTRA TIP…

This method should not be used for unfinished or waxed wood floors. Water should never touch these types of flooring.

LABEL AND STICKY RESIDUE REMOVER

Do you ever buy something special, but when you take the price tag or label off, you are left with an annoying sticky residue? Here is a super-simple solution that works incredibly well.

Yield: ½ cup (118 ml)

2–3 drops lemon essential oil (add more for larger stickers or labels)

½ cup (118 ml) warm water

Remove the sticker or label from the object. Rub several drops of lemon essential oil onto the sticky surface. Work the oil into the residue, then dip a sponge into warm water and wipe it clean.

CARPET STAIN REMOVER (WET AND DRY)

Carpet stains can be hard to tackle. Always try to get them up as soon as they happen, and always blot the stains out; do not rub them unless otherwise instructed. For really stubborn stains, you may need to repeat the following procedure.

Yield: dry & wet stain remover: varies,
foaming carpet stain remover: 5 cups (1 L)

DRY CARPET STAIN REMOVER

Food-grade diatomaceous earth

WET CARPET STAIN REMOVER

Lemon Dish Soap (page 34)

3% food-grade hydrogen peroxide

FOAMING CARPET STAIN REMOVER

2 tbsp (30 ml) liquid castile soap

½ cup (118 ml) hot water

DRY CARPET STAIN REMOVER

If the stain is dry, do not moisten it. Lightly sprinkle diatomaceous earth right on the stain and work it in. Allow it to sit on the stain for 2–3 hours and then vacuum it up.

WET CARPET STAIN REMOVER

Blot the stain out of the carpet as much as possible. Rub a little liquid dish soap into it. When using hydrogen peroxide, it is important to test a small spot to make sure that it isn't harmful to your carpet. If the carpet passes the test, spray the stain liberally with hydrogen peroxide and work it in. Let it sit for 2 minutes and then blot it clean with a hot cloth or towel. Allow to dry. Repeat if necessary.

FOAMING CARPET STAIN REMOVER

In a high-speed blender, add the castile soap and hot water. Blend until a thick foam forms (about 15 seconds). Pour the mixture onto the stain and rub it in. Let it sit for 5 minutes and then blot the stain clean with fresh warm water.

Diatomaceous earth is incredibly absorbent and can pull dirt and stains right out of the carpet. An added bonus is that it also kills critters such as fleas and ants.

CIGARETTE SMOKE ODOR REMOVER

One of the most stubborn smells to get out of a home is cigarette smoke. Clean one room at a time so that the smell does not overwhelm you.

Yield: solution 1: 2 cups (474 ml), solution 2: 1 cup (237 ml)

SOLUTION 1

1 cup (237 ml) water

1 cup (237 ml) vinegar

SOLUTION 2

½ cup (103 g) baking soda

½ cup (103 g) diatomaceous earth

10 drops lemon essential oil (optional)

Start by wiping all the items in the room with Solution 1:

Pour the water and vinegar into a bucket. For walls and ceilings, dampen a cloth in the solution and wipe gently. Heavily polluted walls and ceilings might need to be repainted. Be sure to get all the vents and replace any filters in the room. Wipe down any baseboards, fixtures, cabinets or closet racks.

After the whole space is thoroughly wiped down, treat the carpet with Solution 2:

Combine all of the ingredients in a closed shaker container and shake well to mix. Sprinkle onto the carpet. Let this mixture sit overnight and vacuum it up the following day. If you have other floor surfaces, refer to the General Floor Cleaner recipe on page 59 or to the Wood Floor Cleaner recipe on page 60.

The last step is to pour 1 cup (237 ml) of distilled vinegar into a bowl and place it in the space. Be generous; use three or four bowls. Do not cover or put lids on them. Leave these in the space for up to a month or until the odor has disappeared.

FABRIC UPHOLSTERY FRESHENER

Fabric can become smelly, especially if you have pets in your home. Many turn to upholstery fresheners to rid the fabric of the smell only to find that the smell always comes back, and sometimes it comes back even stronger. Follow this surprisingly effective method to rid your fabric once and for all of odors.

Yield: 1 cup (237 ml)

1 cup (237 ml) distilled vodka

10–20 drops of essential oils (optional)

In a fine mist spray bottle, add the vodka and essential oils, if using. Be sure to test the fabric in an inconspicuous spot to ensure that this solution does not damage it.

Spray the fabric with this solution and let it dry fully. The alcohol will evaporate and help disinfect the fabric, releasing the odor in the process.

FRESH-CUT FLOWER FOOD

It is so wonderful to bring fresh-cut flowers into your home. Once cut, the flowers need nourishment to flourish and last longer. Here is a simple solution that will keep them looking beautiful.

Yield: varies

1 vase full of water

2 tsp (5 g) sugar

1 tsp (5 ml) distilled vodka

Cut the stems of the flowers on a diagonal. Remove all leaves that will be below the water line. In a vase, add the water, sugar and distilled vodka. The vodka helps keep bacteria from growing and will help the flowers last longer. The sugar helps feed the flowers. Replace the water daily for best results.

For fresh-cut flowers, use a little vodka and sugar in the water. The vodka helps keep bacteria from growing and sugar feeds the flowers.

DID YOU KNOW...

Certain flowers can deter wildlife and pests from eating your garden. Try planting marigolds to repel squirrels, passionflowers to repel deer and purple coneflowers to keep the rabbits out of the garden.

Many flowers can be used as food. Try putting pansies or rose petals on your salad. Not only do they bring color to a dish, they actually have a pleasant taste. Many flowers can also be used as medicine. Dandelion flowers are thought to help with digestion, and they make a great addition to any salad.

Flowers are used to make certain essential oils. Essential oils have become wildly popular not only for their cleaning capabilities but also for their healing properties.

CRAYON AND PENCIL MARK REMOVER FOR WALLS

If you have little ones running around your house, it is a sure bet that one day you will be dealing with a crayoned or penciled masterpiece on a wall! Rest assured, there is a super-simple solution that will having you wiping it right off.

Yield: varies

Lemon essential oil

On a damp cloth or sponge, add a few drops of lemon essential oil. Gently rub the crayon or pencil marks until they disappear. That's it! Easy, right?

DID YOU KNOW...

Lemon oil can help in conquering allergies.

Lemon oil can also be used as a safe and natural furniture polish.

Diffused lemon oil can help purify the air that you breathe every day.

LEATHER FURNITURE CLEANER AND CONDITIONER

When cleaning leather furniture, many people turn to a mixture of olive oil and vinegar. Unfortunately, olive oil can damage leather furniture over time, so it is best not to use it. Here is what to do instead. As always, be sure to test a small, inconspicuous spot with this solution to be sure it works with your leather.

Yield: cleaning solution: 1 cup (237 ml), conditioner: 1 polishing cloth

TO CLEAN

½ cup (118 ml) distilled white vinegar

½ cup (118 ml) water

TO CONDITION

15–20 drops lemon essential oil

Vacuum the furniture to remove any dust or dirt. In a bowl, mix together the vinegar and water. Dip part of a clean, soft cloth into the solution so that the cloth is only damp and not really wet. Remember, leather does not like water, so just a slightly damp cloth is best.

Wipe the couch with the damp cloth. Dry the couch fully with a microfiber cloth.

To condition your leather furniture, add 15–20 drops of lemon essential oil to a clean dry cloth. Gently wipe the entire surface with this cloth and watch the shine come out. Lemon oil is considered safe for leather and will help prevent it from cracking.

ELECTRONIC AND TELEVISION SCREEN CLEANER

Today it seems like everyone has computers, tablets, smart phones and larger-than-life televisions. But how do you clean these electronics safely? The solution might surprise you, because once again it is simple.

It is very important to use distilled water. I cannot stress this enough. The minerals in tap water can be damaging to your screen. Also, while many home solutions use alcohol and vinegar to clean screens, they can damage the protective coating that might be on the screen.

Yield: ½ cup (118 ml)

Microfiber cloth

½ cup (118 ml) distilled warm water

Before cleaning any electronics, be sure to turn the power off and allow the screen to cool completely. With a dry microfiber cloth, wipe off any dust or dirt. Be careful not to press too firmly while cleaning.

Add warm distilled water to a spray bottle. Spray just a little onto a soft, dry, lint-free cloth. You want this cloth just slightly damp, not wet. Never spray directly onto any screen: it could damage not only the screen but the entire unit.

Gently clean the surface of the screen with a small, circular motion. If there is a tough stain, do not scratch it off, as this could damage the screen. Just apply this solution several times and let the stain gradually come off. Once the screen is clean, dry it with a dry microfiber cloth and turn the power back on.

FRESHENERS AND DEODORIZERS

Did you know that certain fragrances contain over 100 chemicals? That "fresh scent" air freshener could have a ton of toxic chemicals in it. What's worse, the companies selling these products don't have to disclose any of them. I don't know about you, but I think that is pretty scary.

Commercial candles are another item you want to steer clear of. Why? The fragrances are full of chemicals. When you light the candle, you essentially are releasing chemicals into the air. When you breathe them in, they can cause a variety of health problems. Stick with a clean and simple solution, like using an orange and some olive oil to make a great candle. Can you believe that is all you need to create a beautiful, non-toxic candle? (See page 73 for the recipe.)

One of the most natural ways to freshen up just about anything is with essential oils. Quality essential oils not only smell great, but are antibacterial and can help fight stubborn viruses. I use them whenever possible.

A few other great natural deodorizers are herbs and spices. Common fruits, especially citrus fruit peels, can be combined with herbs and spices to create a great Simmering Potpourri (page 74).

You can easily create a pleasant smell without using one single toxic chemical, and you can be sure that the lovely scent will not be harmful to your health.

CARPET DEODORIZER

Sometimes you just want a room to smell fresh after you clean it. One of the best ways to do that is to sprinkle a little deodorizer onto the carpet. Don't buy commercial deodorizers: they are full of toxic ingredients. A homemade carpet deodorizer is easy to make yourself.

Yield: 2 cups (360 g)

1 cup (205 g) baking soda

1 cup (205 g) diatomaceous earth

15 drops lemon essential oil (optional)

In a medium shaker container, add the baking soda and diatomaceous earth. Add the essential oil, put the lid on and gently shake. Sprinkle onto your carpet and allow to sit for 10–15 minutes. Vacuum the carpet and enjoy the lemony-fresh scent that fills the room.

DID YOU KNOW...

Diatomaceous earth also will kill fleas, lice, cockroaches and ants. If you have animals and you are concerned that you might have fleas, leave this mixture on your carpet overnight and then vacuum. Watch those fleas disappear! Be sure to check out the pest control section starting on page 81 for more ways to get rid of pests.

AIR FRESHENER SPRAY

Here is an easy spray to help freshen up your air.

Yield: 1 cup (237 ml)

¾ cup (177 ml) distilled water

¼ cup (60 ml) vodka

Essential oil combination (see options below)

In a spray bottle, mix together the water and vodka. Use one of the essential oil combinations below for a fresh, clean smell. Spray liberally.

ESSENTIAL OIL COMBINATIONS:

Spring: 5 drops lemon, 5 drops lavender, 5 drops cilantro

Summer: 5 drops wild orange, 5 drops grapefruit, 5 drops lime, 5 drops lemon

Fall: 5 drops cinnamon, 5 drops ginger, 5 drops orange, 1 drop clove

Winter: 5 drops peppermint, 5 drops wintergreen, 5 drops lavender

Holiday: 5 drops peppermint, 5 drops orange, 5 drops cinnamon, 2 drops rosemary

Allergy relief: 8 drops peppermint, 8 drops lavender, 8 drops lemon

Sleep relief: 8 drops lavender, 8 drops roman chamomile, 8 drops wild orange

Focus: 8 drops peppermint, 8 drops cinnamon, 2 drops eucalyptus

BATHROOM AIR FRESHENER

Bathrooms can get stinky fast! Here are several solutions to keep your bathroom smelling fresh.

Yield: reed diffuser: varies on size of vase, scented toilet paper roll: 1 roll, after you poo spray: 2/3 cup (160 ml), easy potpourri: varies

REED DIFFUSER

Small vase

Almond oil

Essential oils

Bamboo skewer sticks

SCENTED TOILET PAPER ROLL

Essential oils

Toilet paper roll

AFTER YOU POO SPRAY

½ cup (118 ml) distilled water

2 tbsp (30 ml) vodka

Essential oils

EASY POTPOURRI

Dried flowers, flower petals and herbs

Essential oils

REED DIFFUSER

To a small vase, add almond oil. Add your favorite essential oils. Lavender, lemon and eucalyptus are all great choices. Add enough to give you the desired scent. Place some bamboo skewer sticks into the vase like they are flowers. The oils will begin to diffuse out of the bamboo sticks and throughout the room.

SCENTED TOILET PAPER ROLL

This one is so simple. Simply place 2 drops (1 on each end) of your favorite essential oil inside the roll of toilet paper, on the cardboard. Every time someone uses toilet paper, the room will automatically be freshened.

AFTER YOU POO SPRAY

In a small spray bottle, mix together the distilled water, vodka and essential oils of choice. Lemon, orange, lime, bergamot and grapefruit are all great choices. Shake well and spray after you're done in the bathroom.

EASY POTPOURRI

Save flowers, flower petals and fresh herbs and dry them for future use. Combine some dried flowers and herbs in a small container and add your favorite essential oils. Cover and let them sit for several weeks. Now transfer the potpourri to an open container and enjoy the scent. You can refresh the essential oils as they dissipate.

Try a few drops of lavender, lemon or orange for a nice fresh scent.

NO-WAX CANDLES

Did you know that you can create a candle with absolutely no wax or even a wick? It can be done, and probably with ingredients you already have in your home! Here's how.

Yield: 1 candle

Large orange or grapefruit

Olive oil

Essential oils (optional)

Cut the fruit in half width-wise, leaving the flower stalk intact. With a knife, gently scrape the fruit inside the circumference to loosen it from the peel. Remove the flesh with a fork, pulling from the center to the edges, leaving in the white center pith.

The intact white pith remaining at the center of the fruit will be your wick. Fill the empty shell with olive oil about ¾ of the way, leaving the center piece of pith (wick) sticking out slightly. Add essential oils if desired. Let the oil sit in the candle for about an hour before you light it.

Place the candle on a heat-resistant surface before lighting it. To light, hold a flame to the wick for about a minute. A long lighter works nicely for this. It might take a little while to light the candle at first, but it will light and your flame will begin to flicker.

FUN FACT...

These candles also float. Try placing them in your bath for a relaxing and uplifting experience.

SIMMERING POTPOURRI

One of the simplest methods for making your house smell amazing is simmering some potpourri. You can be wildly creative with this recipe. Use other spices and herbs that might be in your pantry. Find what smells good to you!

Yield: about 1²/₃ cups (394 ml) each

SPICY SIMMERING POTPOURRI

1½ cups (355 ml) apple cider

1 tbsp (8 g) pumpkin pie spice

½ nutmeg, grated or ½ tsp ground

1 tsp (2 g) cloves

1 cinnamon stick, broken in half

HOLIDAY SIMMERING POTPOURRI

1½ cups (355 ml) water

1–2 sprigs rosemary

¼ cup (25 g) fresh cranberries

Peel of 1 orange or clementine

SPICY SIMMERING POTPOURRI

Mix all the ingredients together and bring to a boil. Reduce heat to the lowest simmer possible. Keep an eye on the simmering potpourri and refill it with more apple cider as needed. Simmer for 2–4 hours or however long you desire.

HOLIDAY SIMMERING POTPOURRI

Mix all the ingredients together and bring to a boil. Reduce heat to the lowest simmer possible. Keep an eye on the simmering potpourri and refill with more water as needed. Simmer for 2–4 hours or however long you desire.

You can easily make your own dry potpourri by drying some flowers, herbs and some dried citrus rinds. To increase the scent, add your favorite essential oils to the potpourri.

REFRIGERATOR DEODORIZER

From time to time, a refrigerator can start to smell, well, not so fresh. A strong odor might be caused by harmful bacteria or molds growing in your fridge, but rest assured that there is a solution for a clean-smelling refrigerator.

Start by clearing everything out of your fridge. Clean the drawers and surface with this solution.

Yield: solution #1: 2 cups (474 ml), solution #2: 1 cup (180 g)

SOLUTION #1

1 cup (237 ml) water

1 cup (237 ml) distilled white vinegar

SOLUTION #2

½ cup (103 g) baking soda

½ cup (103 g) diatomaceous earth

20 drops lemon essential oil

Place Solution 1 ingredients in a spray bottle and liberally spray the entire inside of the refrigerator. Wipe clean and allow to dry. Put everything back into the refrigerator, being careful to wipe off jars and containers. Make sure to throw out any malodorous items.

With a hammer and nail, carefully poke about 8–10 holes in the metal lid of an 8–12 ounce (237–355 ml) mason jar.

Combine all the ingredients for Solution 2 and place them in the mason jar and put the lid on. Place the jar in the refrigerator as a deodorizer. Replace every 1–2 months.

TRASH CAN DEODORIZER

Trash cans are perfect places for odors to collect. A deodorizer is often helpful for fighting them off. Commercial companies often add deodorizers to trash bags, but stay away from them: they are full of chemicals and can make allergies flare up. Try this solution instead.

Yield: 1 cup (237 ml) for spray, about ¼ cup (45 g) for diatomaceous earth

½ cup (118 ml) vinegar

½ cup (118 ml) hot water

Diatomaceous earth

20 drops lemon essential oil

Cotton square

Remove any trash or food that might have been left behind. Wash the trash can by placing the vinegar and hot water in a spray bottle, spraying the surface and wiping clean. Dry the trash can completely. Once it's dry, sprinkle some diatomaceous earth in the bottom. Not only will it help eliminate odor, but it will also kill common bugs, such as roaches, that might go after your trash.

For a fresh, clean smell, add 20 drops of lemon essential oil to a cotton square and place it in the bottom of the trash can. Leave the cotton pad at the bottom of the trash can when removing full trash bags. Replace diatomaceous earth and cotton square every 2 weeks or as needed.

CAR DEODORIZER

Cars can smell sometimes, but they don't have to! Here are several solutions to keep your car smelling fresh and clean.

Yield: mini wooden clothespin vent freshener: 1 clothespin, clay disc or saucer deodorizer: 1 disc, powder air freshener: 1 cup (180 g)

MINI WOODEN CLOTHESPIN VENT FRESHENER

Mini wooden clothespins

Essential oils

CLAY DISC OR SAUCER DEODORIZER

Clay disc or terra-cotta saucer from a small-terra cotta pot

Essential oils

POWDER AIR FRESHENER

½ cup (103 g) baking soda

½ cup (103 g) diatomaceous earth

10 drops lemon essential oil (optional)

MINI WOODEN CLOTHESPIN VENT FRESHENER

Add 5 drops of essential oil to each side of a clothespin, 10 drops total. Clip it to the air vent. When the air or heat comes on, enjoy the fresh scent. Good oils to use are cilantro, lemon, wild orange, eucalyptus, cinnamon and rosemary. Try using a combination of 2 essential oils for a uniquely blended scent.

CLAY DISC OR SAUCER DEODORIZER

Add 10 drops of your favorite essential oil to the clay piece. You can mix the essential oils to create your own blend. Place in the car and replenish oils as needed.

POWDER AIR FRESHENER

With a nail and hammer, carefully poke 8 to 10 holes in the metal lid of an 8–12 ounce (237–355 ml) mason jar. Mix together all the ingredients, place them in the mason jar and put the lid on. Place in the car. Replace the contents of the jar every 1–2 months.

FISH AND BACON ODOR REMOVER

Fish and bacon are delicious, but many people complain that cooking them causes odors that stay in their home. The following key steps can prevent your house from smelling.

• Always use an air vent on high as you cook. Open the windows while cooking.

• Choose the freshest fish possible. Consider poaching or slow baking your fish, and always add lemon and fresh herbs. The lemon helps break down the odor. Try cooking your fish in a pouch that you make from folded parchment paper. The pouch will contain the smell rather than letting it spread through the house.

• When frying bacon, use a spatter screen to contain the oil. Clean up the cooking area immediately afterwards. Consider baking or broiling the bacon to lessen the smell.

• While cooking fish or bacon, place 1 cup (237 ml) of distilled white vinegar or 1 cup (100 g) coffee beans in a container and leave it on the countertop overnight. The vinegar or coffee beans will absorb the strong odor. Discard the next morning.

Yield: about 1¼ cups (300 ml)

1 cup (237 ml) water

3–4 lemon slices, including the peels

6 whole cloves

1 tsp (3 g) cinnamon

Place the ingredients in a small saucepan and bring to a low boil. Reduce the heat to a slight simmer. Simmer for an hour or two or until the smell dissipates. Be careful to watch your solution. If it becomes low on liquid, add a little more water.

Simmering citrus rinds, aromatic herbs and spices can really help eliminate strong odors.

ODOR REMOVER (FOR GARLIC AND ONION ON HANDS)

Garlic and onions leave a smell on your hands that lingers for hours or even into the next day. Here is a quick solution for getting rid of garlic and onion odors left on your hands.

Yield: varies

Soap and water

Stainless steel

1 tsp (5 ml) lemon juice

1 tsp (5 g) coarse kosher salt

4 coffee beans

After you finish handling onions or garlic, wash your hands with soap and water. Be sure to get underneath your fingernails, as the juices can easily get under them. Vigorously rub your hands on something stainless steel, like a sink or faucet or even a large stainless steel spoon. Be sure to get all the areas of the skin that touched the garlic or onions.

Add lemon juice and salt to your hands and rub into your skin. Leave on for 2 minutes and then wash in warm soapy water. Your hands should now be clear of any strong odor. If you still smell garlic or onion on your hands, rub 4 coffee beans vigorously between your hands for 1 minute.

PEST CONTROL

We often think that we have to turn to harmful chemicals to keep pests at bay. This couldn't be further from the truth. Many pests can build up an immunity to common chemicals used by exterminator companies, which is why chemicals are much less effective than we think. Fortunately, there are natural solutions for getting rid of many common pests.

Prevention is your best aid when trying to keep your home free of pests. Always winterize your home. Seal the doors, caulk the windows, replace or repair damaged screens and replace the weatherstripping to make it hard for any creatures to get in.

When you see the first sign of a pest, act fast! Insects can communicate with one another, which often leads to infestation. Once you treat the problem, follow up with several more treatments. In most cases, it takes multiple applications to completely rid your home of a pest.

Get yourself some food-grade diatomaceous earth. This sole ingredient can help you get rid of cockroaches, ants, Asian lady beetles, fleas, bed bugs, centipedes, millipedes and even mice. You can find this at local home improvement stores, pet stores and online.

ASIAN LADY BEETLES

Do you ever see little insects in your home or around the outside of your home that look like ladybugs? These most likely aren't ladybugs but are actually beetles; more specifically, Asian lady beetles.

One way to tell the difference is by the smell. If you pick one up, does it let off a strong odor? If yes, you could have a potential infestation pretty quickly, so act fast. These beetles are very invasive, so tackling them before the problem gets out of hand is very important. Here is how to get rid of them once and for all!

WINTERIZE YOUR HOME

Asian lady beetles come indoors when it gets cold out; then they hibernate. When it starts to warm up in the spring, they come out of hibernation and start searching for food. To stop them from coming in, winterize your home. Seal your doors and windows. Caulk the windows. Replace or repair damaged screens. Replace your weatherstripping.

ACT FAST

Asian lady beetles multiply quickly! They also communicate well with one another by leaving their scent behind, which attracts more Asian lady beetles.

USE FOOD-GRADE DIATOMACEOUS EARTH POWDER

Spread diatomaceous earth powder around the base of your home and in areas of infestation. It effectively kills Asian lady beetles by puncturing their exoskeleton, causing them to dry out and die.

VACUUM THEM UP

If they do make it into your home, vacuum them up quickly with the attachment tools on your vacuum cleaner. The vacuum will not kill them, so be sure to place the vacuum bag in a sealed plastic bag.

ASIAN LADY BEETLES: ELIMINATE THEIR SCENT

Asian lady beetles have a strong odor, which can attract other beetles into your home. They do not like citrus, so use this scent liberally when wiping up after these bugs. After vacuuming, make a spray of citrus oils diluted in some water.

Yield: 2⅛ cups (500 ml)

2 cups (473 ml) water

2 tbsp (30 ml) vodka

30 drops orange essential oil

Mix together all the ingredients in a spray bottle and shake very well. Spray liberally where you see lady beetles.

COCKROACHES

Cockroaches can be problematic to get rid of. They can build up an immunity to chemicals commonly used by exterminator companies. Creating a simple solution at home will safely and quickly get rid of them once and for all. Here are four effective solutions. Keep all of them out of the reach of animals and small children.

Yield: solution #1: varies, solution #2: about 1 tbsp (12 g), solution #3: about ½ cup (48 ml), solution #4: varies

SOLUTION 1

Onion

Large empty spaghetti sauce jar (save the lid for another recipe)

Olive oil

SOLUTION 2

1 tsp (4 g) sugar

3 tsp (13 g) borax

SOLUTION 3

¼ cup (32 g) powdered sugar

¼ cup (52 g) baking soda

1 tbsp (15 ml) juice of choice

SOLUTION 4

Food-grade diatomaceous earth

SOLUTION 1

Slice the onion and place it in the empty jar. Grease the inside of the jar with olive oil to stop the cockroaches from getting out. Place the jar underneath a sink or in other areas where you want to trap cockroaches. Dispose of the roaches once they're captured.

SOLUTION 2

Mix together the ingredients and place in the top of a jar lid, such as a spaghetti sauce jar lid. Place these lids in cabinets or close to the infestation. The sugar will act as bait by attracting cockroaches, and the borax will kill them.

SOLUTION 3

Mix together the ingredients to form a thick paste. Place about 1 tablespoon (15 ml) in a small bowl or the lid of a jar. The sugar will act as bait by attracting cockroaches, and the baking soda will kill them.

SOLUTION 4

With a duster, dust food-grade diatomaceous earth inside cabinets in the cracks and crevices. This should be a light dusting, as a little goes a long way.

Sprinkle food-grade diatomaceous earth around the perimeter of your home to keep roaches from entering. The diatomaceous earth effectively kills cockroaches by puncturing their exoskeletons, which causes them to dry out and die.

FLEAS

Fleas can quickly take over a space if they aren't dealt with quickly. If you are experiencing fleas, it is important to treat your yard, your pets and your home. Contact a holistic veterinarian for advice on how to naturally get rid of fleas on your pets. Here is the simple solution for your home.

Vacuum the entire house, including furniture, under furniture and beds. If an animal sleeps in bed with you, remove the sheets and vacuum the entire bed. Be sure to get under the mattress and around the box spring. Dispose of the vacuum bag. Wash all the bedding of pets, including the sheets if the animal sleeps in bed with you.

Yield: varies

---

1 cup (206 g) food-grade diatomaceous earth (plus more if needed)

Sifter

Place the diatomaceous earth in the sifter and sift a small amount onto all your carpets. Leave on for 24–48 hours, then vacuum up. Be sure to treat the bedding or any areas where the pet sleeps. The diatomaceous earth will kill the fleas within 6 hours, but it will not kill the flea eggs.

It is important to follow up by using this method once a week until all fleas that hatch are killed and eliminated. This could take up to a month.

For the yard, liberally sprinkle diatomaceous earth throughout the grass and around bushes, flower beds and trees, making sure to cover all areas. Repeat weekly until you get rid of the fleas. Keep fleas to a minimum by applying diatomaceous earth once a month.

SAFETY NOTES...

Diatomaceous earth is a fine powder that is safe for humans and pets but can cause issues for those with sensitive lungs. Wearing a mask while sifting the diatomaceous earth onto the carpet and in your yard can protect you from getting too much dust in your system. After it has settled, you no longer need the mask.

Always buy food-grade diatomaceous earth and not pool-grade diatomaceous earth.

FRUIT FLIES

The warm summer months bring delicious ripe fruits! Unfortunately, ripe fruits can also bring abundant fruit flies. Here are several steps to help you get rid of them.

First, eliminate what is bringing fruit flies into your home. Check to make sure you have no rotten fruit or vegetables. Don't leave out dirty dishes or half-full glasses of fruit juice or other sugary drinks. Thoroughly clean the area that has fruit flies. Certain bacteria can attract fruit flies, so a good cleaning is helpful.

To capture the fruit flies currently in your home, create a trap.

Yield: about ½ cup (118 ml)

½ cup (118 ml) apple cider vinegar

1 tsp (5 ml) Lemon Dish Soap
(page 34)

16 oz (473 ml) plastic cup or glass jar

A funnel, or else a sheet of paper or paper plate made into a funnel (you will need to discard it)

Place the vinegar and dish soap in the cup or jar. Make a funnel if necessary. Place the funnel into the cup so that it isn't touching the surface of the liquid, but it leads the fruit flies into the cup. Place the trap in the area where the fruit flies are located. Dispose of the trap once all fruit flies are trapped.

The sweetness of apple cider vinegar is what attracts fruit flies to this trap. Avoid using distilled white vinegar because it is not as sweet.

ANT CONTROL

Ants can be a nuisance, especially in the home. When at all possible, eliminate the ants at their source. Keep crumbs off of countertops and floors. Here's an easy way to get rid of ants.

Yield: inside the home: 1 ant trap, outside the home: varies

INSIDE THE HOME

1 tbsp (8 g) powdered sugar

1 tbsp (13 g) baking soda

OUTSIDE THE HOME

1 (96-oz [3-L]) kettle boiling water

Diatomaceous earth

ANT CONTROL INSIDE THE HOME

For inside the home, simply create an ant trap.

Place the powdered sugar and baking soda in a lid or saucer. Place these in the areas where you see ants. The sugar will attract the ants and the baking soda will kill them.

ANT CONTROL OUTSIDE THE HOME

If you can find the anthill, you can eliminate the whole colony at one time. Here's how.

Pour one kettle of boiling water down the hole of the anthill. Wait 5 minutes and repeat if necessary. You will have a few stragglers who were out getting food; you can get rid of these with a trap or by using diatomaceous earth.

To keep the ants from entering the home, use food-grade diatomaceous earth around the perimeter. Simply sprinkle it around the base of your home. The diatomaceous earth effectively kills ants by puncturing their exoskeletons, which causes them to dry out and die.

BED BUGS

A bed bug infestation doesn't mean you are dirty. You might simply have picked them up from a hotel room or other public setting.

Many think the best way to get rid of bed bugs is with toxic chemicals, but there are more effective and natural ways. It is important to follow all these steps to effectively get rid of bed bugs.

Yield: varies

Food-grade diatomaceous earth

Remove all linens and wash them in hot water. Use a sanitize cycle if you have it on your washing machine. Dry the linens on the hottest heat setting, and if you have a sanitize cycle on your dryer, use it. Meanwhile, pull the bed away from any walls. Vacuum your entire bed, including all the crevasses and cracks. Vacuum the baseboards and any areas near the bed.

Vacuum the box spring, if you have one. Vacuum under the bed and under any bedposts. If the bed is on a stand, be sure to vacuum the stand. Take it apart, if needed, to clean all areas where bed bugs could be hiding. Be sure to vacuum the entire room and dispose of any vacuum bags right away.

Sprinkle diatomaceous earth around the entire room, including carpets, bed springs and mattresses, and under furniture and on pillows. Be sure to get the diatomaceous earth in all the corners, nooks and crannies. Bed bugs cannot fly, so be sure to generously sprinkle around the posts of the bed, so any bed bugs coming back to the bed will be destroyed.

Repeat this once a week for 1 month or until all the bed bugs are gone.

Diatomaceous earth does not lose its effectiveness over time like chemicals. It is important to continue treatment until all the eggs have hatched and the hatchlings are destroyed and eliminated. Diatomaceous earth effectively kills bed bugs by puncturing their exoskeletons, which causes them to dry out and die.

HORNETS AND WASPS

Getting rid of hornets and wasps is quite easy. I am not a fan of traps, because you want to be sure not to capture honeybees. Honeybees are essential to our food chain because they pollinate fruits and vegetables.

To eliminate wasps and hornets, try to attack them at their source. If the nest is large, it is best to call the professionals to remove it. If the nest is small, see the solution below. If you wish to get rid of wasps and hornets in smaller areas, mix up this solution and they will be gone in no time.

Yield: 1 ³/₄ cup (414 ml) for spray, diatomaceous earth: varies

1 cup (237 ml) water

½ cup (118 ml) isopropyl rubbing alcohol or vodka

¼ cup (60 ml) Lemon Dish Soap (page 34)

Food-grade diatomaceous earth

Mix together the water, alcohol and dish soap. Spray onto hornets or wasps. They should fall to the ground immediately and die.

To get rid of small nests, sprinkle diatomaceous earth on the nest at dusk when the hornets and wasps are less active. Be sure to wear long pants and a long-sleeved shirt, covering as much of your body as possible. Repeat this 2–3 times over the next few days until you notice that the hornets and wasps are gone.

Hornets and wasps can be quite a nuisance. When getting rid of them, take extra precautions to not harm honeybees. Honeybees pollinate fruits and vegetables and are essential to our food chain.

CENTIPEDES AND MILLIPEDES

Centipedes and millipedes are long creatures with a ton of legs, which allow them to move really fast! They don't usually travel in large groups, so they are usually easy to get rid of.

Centipedes and millipedes like damp places. It is common to see them in bathrooms, garages and basements. If you see one, spray it immediately with this solution.

Yield: 1 cup (237 ml)

1 cup (237 ml) isopropyl rubbing alcohol or vodka

20 drops eucalyptus essential oil

Spray directly on the insects as soon as you see them.

To prevent them from entering your house in the first place, be sure to seal your doors and windows. Caulk the windows and replace weatherstripping if needed. Remove any wood piles, compost piles or any other organic matter that is likely to stay moist.

Keep your home dry. Consider getting a dehumidifier for any damp areas. Spread food-grade diatomaceous earth around the base of your home. It effectively kills centipedes and millipedes by puncturing their exoskeletons, which causes them to dry out and die.

MICE

If you have mice, you probably understand how difficult it can be to get rid of them. There are several steps to prevent them from coming into your home in the first place.

First, do a thorough walk-through of your home to find holes where they might be coming in. Check behind the stove, under the kitchen sink, by the gas lines, under the radiators and in the garage. Pay close attention to the basement if you have one. Tightly pack any holes with fine steel wool and seal them off with a spray foam. Be sure to seal your doors and windows. Caulk the windows and replace weatherstripping if needed to make it hard for any creatures to get in.

Next, make a solution to deter mice from coming back. Mice don't typically like peppermint oil, so here's one to try.

Yield: ¼ cup (45 g)

½ cup (103 g) diatomaceous earth

1 tbsp (15 ml) water

15 drops peppermint essential oil

Empty lids

Place the diatomaceous earth in a container. Add the water and peppermint essential oil and stir well. It will have a crumbly texture.

Place about 1 tablespoon (13 g) of the mixture onto empty lids and place around the home. It is important to note that diatomaceous earth and essential oils will not kill rodents. Diatomaceous earth acts as an absorbent. Adding water and essential oils creates a powerful and highly absorbent substance. The strong smell deters mice from coming into the home, sending them on their way.

If this solution starts to lose its peppermint smell, add a little more water and a few more drops of essential oil to freshen it up.

OUTDOORS

Even though the cleaning is happening outside the home, it's not okay to use toxic chemicals. Our children play outdoors, our pets roll around and run in the yard. It is just as important to use nontoxic ingredients outdoors as it is indoors.

Two places to consider using nontoxic ingredients are the patio and the grilling area. You can easily get rid of weeds between pavers with boiling water instead of toxic chemicals. Need a heavy degreaser for the grill? Use the solution on page 97, which is safe for any grill and will work better than any commercial cleaner.

Do you have a garden? Don't spray it with harmful chemicals. Try making a natural garden pesticide spray and watch your garden flourish. Want to get rid of weeds in your garden or yard? Check out the weed control solutions on page 95.

Let's not forget about car care. No need to use toxic chemicals there either. Learn how to naturally de-ice a car (page 99), wash and clean your car (page 98) and even how to naturally wax your car (page 98), all with only a few quality natural ingredients.

BUG SPRAY AND PATIO DIFFUSER REPELLENT

Bugs can be bothersome while you're trying to enjoy outside activities. Most bug repellents on the market today are filled with toxic chemicals and other undesirable ingredients. The good news is that there are natural remedies to help keep pesky bugs at bay.

Yield: mosquito and gnat spray: 1 cup (237 ml), outdoor patio diffuser repellent: varies

MOSQUITO AND GNAT SPRAY

½ cup (118 ml) witch hazel

½ cup (118 ml) vodka (omit for children and use more witch hazel)

15 drops eucalyptus essential oil

15 drops lemongrass essential oil

15 drops citronella essential oil

5 drops rosemary essential oil

OUTDOOR PATIO DIFFUSER REPELLENT

Water

2 drops citronella essential oil

2 drops lemongrass essential oil

2 drops grapefruit essential oil

1 drop clove essential oil

MOSQUITO AND GNAT SPRAY

In a small spray bottle, combine the witch hazel and vodka and mix well. Add the eucalyptus, lemongrass, citronella and rosemary. Shake well.

To use, spray a small amount on your skin and clothes. Repeat as needed.

OUTDOOR PATIO DIFFUSER REPELLENT

Diffusers aren't just for indoors; they can be taken outside too. If you don't have a diffuser for the outdoors, consider purchasing a portable one that has rechargeable batteries and uses a cold water mist to diffuse the oils.

Add the recommended water amount for your specific diffuser. Add the essential oils and begin diffusing in the area where people are gathering.

WEED KILLER

Weeds can be such a nuisance! There are several safe and all-natural alternatives for killing weeds. Here are a few.

Yield: driveway cracks, paving stones & sidewalks: varies on size, kill weeds in grass: about 1 gallon (4 L), in the garden: varies on size of garden

DRIVEWAY CRACKS, PAVING STONES AND SIDEWALKS

Water

KILL WEEDS IN GRASS

1 gallon (4 L) 10% white distilled vinegar (100 grain)

2 tbsp (30 ml) Lemon Dish Soap (page 34)

1 tbsp (15 ml) liquid molasses

IN THE GARDEN

Newspaper

WEED KILLER FOR DRIVEWAY CRACKS, PAVING STONES AND SIDEWALKS

Boil some water and pour directly over the weed. Be careful to pour 1–2 inches (2.5–5 cm) above the crown of the weed and pour slowly so that the water doesn't splash on you. The weeds will die within a day or two.

KILL WEEDS IN GRASS

Combine these ingredients in a weed sprayer and spot-treat the weeds in your yard. Do not spray the entire grass area, as this will kill the grass; just spot-treat the weeds. The weeds will die in a few days. Repeat as needed.

WEED KILLER IN THE GARDEN

Lay newspapers over the weeds. Dampen the papers lightly so they don't blow away. The lack of light will eventually kill the weeds without harming your fruits, vegetables and herbs. Don't worry about removing the newspapers; they will naturally break down into the soil.

NATURAL GARDEN PESTICIDE

One of the most rewarding experiences is growing your own organic food. It can be challenging, but it is well worth the effort. One of the most frustrating parts of gardening is dealing with pests, specifically aphids, beetle grubs, squash bugs and ants. Here is a nontoxic solution safe for even organic gardens.

Yield: 4 cups (946 ml)

4 cups (496 ml) water

2 tbsp (26 g) diatomaceous earth

2 drops garlic essential oil

2 drops onion essential oil

2 drops peppermint essential oil

4 drops melaleuca (tea tree) essential oil

Place all the ingredients in a 32-ounce (947-ml) spray bottle and shake well. Spray on all the plants in the early morning. Avoid using this solution in peak sun times. The solution will dry on the plants, creating a light, powdery dust. This is the diatomaceous earth doing its magic.

The diatomaceous earth will effectively kill any pests that have an exoskeleton, while the garlic, onion, peppermint and melaleuca essential oils will deter other pests without exoskeletons, including unwanted fungi.

For further protection, diatomaceous earth powder can be lightly sprinkled around the base of the plants.

Onion and garlic deter many critters from invading your garden. Garlic helps keep insects and deer away and onions keep aphids, moles and rabbits from entering your garden.

HEAVY-DUTY GRILL CLEANER

Cleaning a grill is a dirty job; there is no way around it. The key to a clean grill is having a heavy-duty degreaser that cuts through all the layers of built-up grease. It is important to use hot water when cleaning the grill. It will help you cut through the grease and will leave your grill looking like new again.

Yield: spray solution: 2 ¾ cups (650 ml), water solution: about 1 gallon (4 L)

1½ cups (355 ml) warm distilled water

2 tsp (10 g) kosher salt

¾ cup (155 g) Dr. Bronner's Sal Suds

½ cup (118 ml) vinegar

1 gallon (4 L) hot water

1 tbsp (15 ml) Lemon Dish Soap (page 34)

In a medium bowl, add the warm distilled water and dissolve the kosher salt. Do not leave the salt out; this thickens the degreaser. Stir in the Sal Suds and vinegar and stir lightly. Pour into a spray bottle. To use, spray directly on the grill. This solution is safe for all areas of the grill. Be sure to get the inside and outside of the grill, the grates and the drip pans.

In a large, 3-gallon (11-L) bucket, add the hot water and liquid dish soap. With a sponge and some elbow grease, rub the solution into the surface, going with the grain of the stainless steel. For tough stains, allow the solution to sit for 5–10 minutes before you rinse it off. Rinse the solution off the entire grill and dry with a clean towel.

SCREEN CLEANER

Window screens can be a pain to clean, but with a couple of key ingredients you can clean them in no time. Here is what you need.

Yield: about 2 gallons (7.5 L) and 1 cup (237 ml)

2 gallons (8 L) hot water

1 tbsp (15 ml) Lemon Dish Soap (page 34)

1 cup (237 ml) 3% food-grade hydrogen peroxide

Add the ingredients to a 3-gallon (11-L) bucket. Dip a nylon scrub brush into the solution and rub it gently onto the screen. Gently scrub. The screen will be soapy. Allow the screen to sit for 5 minutes with the soap mixture on and then rinse clean.

CAR WASH SOAP

We all want our cars to look like new! Taking your car to the car wash once a week can get expensive. Washing your car at your home is much more cost-effective, and your car usually comes out cleaner, too!

Yield: about 1 gallon (4 L)

1 gallon (4 L) warm water

1 tbsp (15 ml) Lemon Dish Soap (page 34)

Mix the water and dish soap together. Dip a large sponge into the soapy water and begin cleaning the surface of your car. For hard-to-clean areas such as bumpers and tires, use a nylon brush. Also use the brush to get bugs and other foreign substances off of the vehicle. Follow up with a perfect car wax (see below) to make your car shine.

WAX FOR CARS

After washing your car, adding a layer of wax can really bring the shine back. There is no need to buy car waxes with toxic ingredients; you can easily make one in your own home. Here is a simple solution for waxing your car naturally.

Yield: about 1/2 cup (80 g)

¼ cup (55 g) coconut oil

¼ cup (60 ml) almond oil

1 tbsp (11 g) + 1 tsp (4 g) carnauba wax

2 tsp (7 g) beeswax

20 drops orange essential oil

In a double boiler, melt the coconut oil. Use a glass mason jar or old metal can in the double boiler. Do note that once you use the jar or can, the wax will not come out of it, so it is best to designate one jar or can for all future use. Once the oil is melted, add in almond oil, carnauba wax and beeswax and continue to heat over a double boiler until fully melted (about 3 minutes).

Remove the container from the heat source and let it sit for 2 minutes. Add in the orange essential oil and swirl until well blended. Pour immediately into a shallow glass jar (if not using one already) and let it set. This wax should be ready to use in an hour or two.

To use the wax, make sure your car is washed and free of any dirt, bugs and other foreign substances. With a clean, lint-free cloth, wipe on the wax in a circular motion. Leave it on for 10 minutes. With a clean, dry, lint-free cloth, buff the wax off in a circular motion. Your car will be shiny and will look like you just drove it off a new car lot!

CAR DE-ICER

When it's cold out, the last thing you want to do is stand outside, chipping away at the ice that has accumulated on your car's windshield or in your car's locks. Haven't you wondered whether there's an easier solution for quickly and effectively getting rid of ice?

Guess what, there is! Follow this simple solution and watch the ice melt within seconds, right before your eyes!

Yield: 4 cups (946 ml)

3 cups (710 ml) isopropyl rubbing alcohol (91% or higher works best)

1 cup (237 ml) water

Combine the alcohol and water in a large spray bottle. Spray the solution on the iced windshield and locks. The ice will instantly start to melt. Store the bottle in the trunk of your car as the alcohol will prevent it from freezing.

DID YOU KNOW...

Rock salt and other salts used to de-ice roads, driveways and sidewalks are very corrosive to concrete, roads, cars, metals and plant life. Consider using magnesium chloride to melt away the ice. It is much less corrosive on concrete, metals and roads and it won't hurt your plants, animals or carpets.

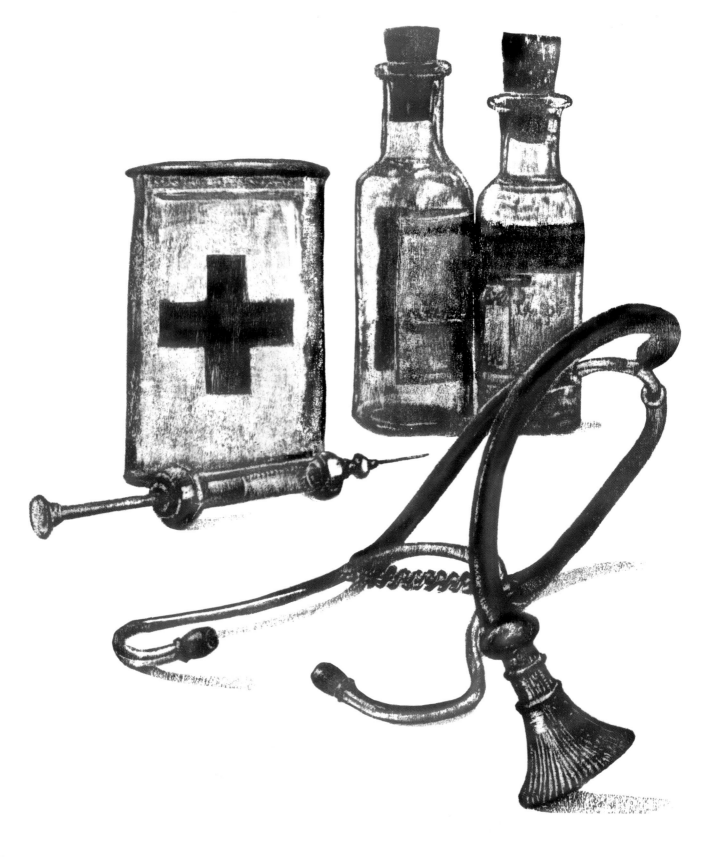

PART TWO

NATURAL SOLUTIONS FOR COMMON HEALTH PROBLEMS

HEAD, EARS FACE AND MOUTH

This chapter focuses on natural remedies for common problems of the head, ears, face and mouth.

Do you struggle with headaches? Do you often reach for over-the-counter pain medication? Over-the-counter pain medications have some pretty terrible side effects. There are natural remedies to treat migraines, tension headaches and even sinus headaches (page 104).

Did you know that some common toothpastes on the market can actually be harmful for your teeth? With a couple of ingredients, you can make an effective and simple toothpaste (page 118).

How great would it be to have to wash your hair less? There is a dry shampoo (page 105) that you can use daily, which will reduce the number of times you have to wash your hair to 1–2 times a week. You can customize this shampoo for dry hair, dull hair, oily hair, dandruff, thinning hair and even for lice prevention.

Do you suffer from styes or pinkeye? You will be amazed by how easy they are to get rid of with simple ingredients you probably already have in your home (pages 111–112).

How about ear infections? Do you get them often? What about swimmer's ear? Did you know you can prevent swimmer's ear with only two ingredients (page 114)?

Dealing with cold sores or canker sores can be so bothersome! Start healing them quickly and naturally with a few easy steps (pages 120–121)!

HEADACHES AND MIGRAINES

All too often, we reach for over-the-counter pain medications when we have headaches. These medications carry a long list of side effects that include damaging the liver or even causing kidney problems. Thankfully, there are essential oils that can help us get rid of headaches.

If you are new to any of these essential oils, be sure to always dilute them with a carrier oil (such as coconut, almond, jojoba or olive oil), and test a small section of your skin to make sure that you don't have a reaction to that particular oil.

Yield: migraine headache: 1-oz (30-ml) roller bottle, sinus headache: 1-oz (30-ml) roller bottle, tension headache: 1-oz (30-ml) roller bottle

MIGRAINE HEADACHE

6 drops peppermint oil

4 drops lavender oil

2 drops wintergreen oil

2 tbsp (30 ml) carrier oil (coconut oil, jojoba oil, almond oil or olive oil)

SINUS HEADACHE

6 drops peppermint oil

6 drops eucalyptus oil

2 tbsp (30 ml) carrier oil (coconut oil, jojoba oil, almond oil or olive oil)

TENSION HEADACHE

4 drops eucalyptus

4 drops peppermint oil

2 drops cilantro oil

2 drops rosemary oil

2 tbsp (30 ml) carrier oil (coconut oil, jojoba oil, almond oil or olive oil)

MIGRAINE HEADACHE

Migraine headaches are some of the most severe headaches. They can cause blurred vision, extreme sensitivity to light, anxiety and nausea.

Combine all the ingredients in a 1-ounce (30-ml) roller bottle. Roll a few times on the temples, forehead and back of the neck.

SINUS HEADACHE

Sinus headaches can be caused by inflammation or infection in the sinus passage. Common conditions that cause a sinus headache are respiratory infection, allergies and cold or flu.

Combine all the ingredients in a 1-ounce (30-ml) roller bottle. Roll a few times onto the chest, under the nose and on the temples.

TENSION HEADACHE

Tension headaches are often caused by stress. They are associated with a dull, constant pain in the head and neck and behind the eyes. Taking a bath with lavender oil can help reduce tension.

Combine all the ingredients in a 1-ounce (30-ml) roller bottle. Rub a few times onto the temples, forehead, wrists and the back of the neck.

HEALING AND NOURISHING CUSTOMIZABLE DRY SHAMPOO

For dandruff, dry hair, fragile hair, oily hair, hair growth, hair loss and lice prevention!

Have you ever wanted a product that would allow you to shower less and still have non-greasy, bouncy hair? This is that product. With a few simple ingredients, you can customize a blend of dry shampoo that is perfect for your hair. This recipe is safe for color-treated hair.

Yield: about ¼ cup (45 g)

¼ cup (56 g) arrowroot powder

If you have dark hair: 2–3 tsp (5–7 g) cocoa powder

If you have medium-colored hair: 2–3 tsp (5–7 g) ground cinnamon

If you have light hair: 1–2 tsp (2.5–5 g) ground nutmeg

If you have gray or white hair: no need to add any coloring

2–3 drops of essential oils for your hair type (optional); see guide to the right

In a small container (preferably one that has a shaker lid on top), add the arrowroot powder. Add the optional cocoa, cinnamon or nutmeg to match your hair color. Add your choice of essential oils and shake until well blended.

Place a very small amount—about a dime size—into your hands and rub together. Apply the powder to dry hair at the roots, right at the scalp. Style as usual.

Dry shampoo works best on days 2–4 of unwashed hair.

By adding a few drops of essential oils to this natural dry shampoo recipe, you can customize it to fit your needs. Here are some ways to improve your hair with essential oils:

Dandruff: 2–3 drops lavender or wintergreen

Dry hair: 2–3 drops geranium, sandalwood or lavender

Fragile hair: 2–3 drops sage, lavender or thyme

Greasy or oily hair: 2–3 drops basil, cypress, thyme, lemon or rosemary

Growth (to stimulate): 2–3 drops thyme, lavender or rosemary

Itching: 2–3 drops peppermint

Hair loss: 2–3 drops rosemary, lavender or thyme

Head lice prevention: 2–3 drops of eucalyptus, rosemary or melaleuca (tea tree)

ALL-NATURAL HEAD LICE TREATMENT

Having lice doesn't mean you are dirty; these bugs can cling to any hair. "Super lice" is a new strain that is resistant to common chemicals used to treat lice outbreaks. We're fortunate that there is a natural solution that can get rid of them once and for all.

Yield: lice powder: ¼ cup (52 g), lice protective spray: 1 cup (237 ml)

¼ cup (52 g) food-grade diatomaceous earth

10 drops melaleuca essential oil (tea tree oil)

1 cup (237 ml) witch hazel

10 drops eucalyptus essential oil

10 drops rosemary essential oil

Mix together the diatomaceous earth and tea tree essential oil. Place a small amount in your hands and massage into the hair and scalp. Make sure to cover all areas. Diatomaceous earth can create a lot of dust, so you may want to put a mask on the person's mouth and nose while applying.

Leave on the hair overnight. Wash the hair the next morning and dry it with a blow dryer. Use a lice comb to remove any eggs or nits.

Make a preventative spray of 1 cup (237 ml) witch hazel and 10 drops eucalyptus plus 10 drops rosemary essential oils. Liberally spray daily on dry or wet hair, then style as usual.

Repeat the same process for two more days or as needed.

Certain plant oils may work to help prevent lice. Several of these oils are rosemary, citronella, tea tree, eucalyptus and lemongrass.

DID YOU KNOW...

Diatomaceous earth effectively kills lice by puncturing their exoskeletons, which causes them to dry out and die.

NOURISHING HAIR MASK

Sometimes your hair just needs a little special attention. Apply these masks to your hair as needed, usually about every 2 weeks.

Yield: all hairtypes: ¼–½ cup (60–115 ml), dull or limp hair: ½ cup + 12 oz beer (410 ml), itchy scalp: about 2 tbsp (30 ml), dry or sun-damaged hair: ⅓ cup (78 ml)

ALL HAIR TYPES

1–2 eggs

DULL OR LIMP HAIR

½ cup (55 g) organic mayonnaise or full-fat plain Greek yogurt

12 oz (355 ml) can of beer

ITCHY SCALP

1 tbsp (15 ml) lemon juice

2 tsp (10 ml) jojoba oil

3 drops lavender essential oil

DRY OR SUN-DAMAGED HAIR

⅓ cup (78 ml) honey

ALL HAIR TYPES MASK

Eggs are one of the most nourishing ingredients to use on hair. The yolks help moisturize and the whites help reduce unwanted oil.

Crack eggs into a blender and blend well. Place in a squeeze bottle and generously squeeze onto dry hair, starting at the scalp and working your way to the ends. Leave on for 20 minutes and then rinse in cool water. Shampoo and condition your hair as usual.

DULL OR LIMP HAIR MASK

If you use a lot of products in your hair, the shine in your hair can disappear. Add some life back with a little yogurt or mayonnaise.

Place either mayonnaise or yogurt in a bowl and rub into your dry hair. Start at the scalp and work your way down to the ends. Leave in for 20 minutes and then rinse with warm water. Shampoo and condition your hair as usual. For extra shine and volume, do a final rinse with a can of beer. Pour the beer liberally into hair, leave in for 2–3 minutes and then rinse out.

ITCHY SCALP MASK

Hair often changes with the seasons. In cooler climates, the scalp can become dry and flaky, so a little extra moisture can do wonders.

Mix together lemon juice, jojoba oil and lavender oil and massage onto a dry scalp. Leave the mixture in for 20 minutes, then shampoo and condition your hair as usual.

DRY OR SUN-DAMAGED HAIR MASK

Honey is one of the most nourishing foods that you can put on your hair. It naturally locks in moisture and can help repair damaged hair.

Simply rub honey into your dry hair. Start at the scalp and work your way down to the ends. Leave in for 20 minutes and then rinse. Shampoo and condition your hair as usual.

LIGHTEN HAIR NATURALLY

You don't need the harsh chemicals of bleach to color your hair. You can safely lighten your hair naturally with lemon juice, chamomile tea and the sun. You can make highlights or lighten your whole head. For best results, follow this treatment with a nourishing hair mask of your choice on page 107.

Yield: 5 cups (1 L)

8 tea bags organic chamomile tea

4 cups (946 ml) boiling water

1 cup (237 ml) lemon juice

Add the tea bags to the boiling water and let steep for 20 minutes. Remove the tea bags and stir in the lemon juice. Allow the mixture to cool, then pour it into a spray bottle. Spray dry strands of hair for highlights or your entire dry head for full coverage. Spray liberally; you want the hair that you are treating to be fully saturated with this solution.

Go out into the sun and allow the sun to fully dry your hair. This can take anywhere from 1–2 hours. Your hair will gradually lighten. If you prefer to lighten it more, repeat this method several times over the next few weeks.

Lemon alone gradually lightens hair over time with the help of the sun. Adding chamomile tea will lighten hair much faster, often within several hours.

DARKEN HAIR NATURALLY

The best way to color dark hair is with henna. Henna (Lawsonia inermis) is a flowering plant that is found in the desert. The leaves of this plant have a coloring pigment called lawsone. The leaves are crushed into a fine powder, which creates a natural dye for coloring light brown to dark brown hair. Water, lemon juice or vinegar is added to create a paste to apply to the hair.

Henna is a permanent color for the hair. It will last up to 3 months. It will not lighten your hair; it can only make it darker and will often add a red tint. You can purchase henna online in bulk, or you can get it from a quality health food store. Typically, 6 ounces (177 g) of henna is all you need. If you have extremely long hair, you might need a bit more; or if your hair is very short, you might need a bit less. Make sure you buy for your current color of hair. Do not use henna if you have blond hair or a lot of gray hair. Be sure to pick up a pair of disposable rubber gloves, as henna stains everything.

Yield: varies depending on length of hair

6 oz (177 g) henna

Boiling water

Coconut oil

Place the henna in a disposable plastic container and add enough boiling water to create a smooth and thick consistency. Depending on which brand of henna you buy, you might need to add lemon juice or apple cider vinegar.

Wipe the coconut oil around the rim of your hairline, around your face and around your ears. This will help prevent the henna from staining your skin. Wearing disposable gloves, divide your hair into 1-inch (2.5-cm) sections and brush the henna onto the hair. Start at the scalp and work your way down to the tips of your hair. Continue until all your hair is covered. Wipe off any excess henna with a cotton ball.

Cover your hair with plastic wrap or a plastic shower cap and allow the color to sit for 45–120 minutes. Check a strand of hair after 45 minutes. Once you reach the desired color, rinse out the henna with warm water. Shampoo and condition your hair as you normally would and finish with a cool water rinse. Henna naturally fades after 4–6 weeks. It is safe to color again with henna after this time.

DID YOU KNOW...

Henna naturally conditions the hair and can help get rid of dandruff. Henna has been used for many years as medicine. It is thought to have anti-bacterial and anti-fungal properties. Many people who suffer from psoriasis find that henna can help reduce redness, flaking and itchiness of the scalp.

DANDRUFF CONTROL

Dandruff appears on the scalp in the form of loose skin or flakes. It can be extremely itchy and can often lead to other problematic issues. Signs of dandruff include tightness or a hot feeling on the scalp, white flakes that fall out of your hair and onto your shoulders, itchy scalp and a red rash or red patches on the scalp.

If you are experiencing any of these, consider taking a look at your diet, because diet can contribute to dandruff problems. Try eliminating inflammatory foods and processed foods and add more vegetables and fruits.

Yield: ¼ cup (60 ml)

2 tbsp (30 ml) apple cider vinegar

2 tbsp (30 ml) water

5 drops of melaleuca (tea tree) essential oil or oregano essential oil

Mix together the apple cider vinegar with water and pour it into a spray bottle. Add 5 drops of melaleuca oil or oregano oil to the mixture.

Shake and spritz on your scalp. Wrap your hair in a towel and allow it to sit for 30–45 minutes.

Rinse well and style as usual. Repeat if needed up to 2 times a week.

DID YOU KNOW...

Melaleuca and oregano essential oils have antibacterial, antiviral and anti-fungal properties that can help treat dandruff and reduce inflammation. Apple cider vinegar has healing properties, too. Real apple cider vinegar is a fermented liquid that is full of probiotics and beneficial bacteria.

STYE

A stye (also known as hordeolum) is a red bump located near the edge of the eye. It can look like a pimple and often has a liquid or pus oozing from it. Never squeeze a stye. Don't put makeup on it and keep the area clean. Styes are usually not an emergency and often can be treated with home remedies.

Here are a few methods to help get rid of a stye.

Yield: green tea: 1 tea bag, ground turmeric: ¼ tsp, castor oil: 1 drop, warm compress: 1 compress, pure aloe vera: varies

GREEN TEA

1 green tea bag

Boiling water

GROUND TURMERIC

½ tsp turmeric (preferably organic)

Water

CASTOR OIL

1 drop castor oil

WARM COMPRESS

Clean washcloth

PURE ALOE VERA

Aloe vera

SAFETY NOTE . . .

Styes typically go away on their own within a week, but if you are still experiencing discomfort after a few days of treatment, or if the stye gets worse, seek medical attention.

GREEN TEA

Green tea has tannins that can help get rid of styes. Green tea can also help reduce inflammation. Dip a tea bag into boiling water and remove it from the heat. Allow it to cool to warm temperature. Place the tea bag on the eye that has the stye. Leave the tea bag on for 10 minutes. Repeat 2–3 times a day until the stye is gone.

GROUND TURMERIC

Turmeric is one of the most powerful natural anti-inflammatory agents for fighting a stye. Place turmeric in a bowl and add a little water to create a thick paste. Apply to the stye and allow it to dry fully. Leave this mixture on the stye for 10 minutes. Remove the turmeric with a warm wash cloth. Repeat 1–2 times a day until the stye is gone.

CASTOR OIL

Castor oil has been used for hundreds of years as medicine. It has antibacterial properties that can help get rid of a stye. Add castor oil to the stye 2–3 times a day. Follow up with a warm compress on the eye for 15 minutes.

WARM COMPRESS

Sometimes all you need is a warm compress to help reduce the swelling and clear up a stye. Soak a clean washcloth in some warm water. Place it on the eye that has the stye. Allow it to sit for 10–15 minutes. Repeat 2–3 times a day.

PURE ALOE VERA

Aloe vera is nature's natural anti-inflammatory and has antibacterial properties. Use pure aloe vera by removing the gel from the leaves or you can use pure organic aloe vera. To use, place a small amount of gel onto the stye and allow it to sit on the stye for 30 minutes. Rinse and repeat 3–5 times a day.

PINKEYE

Pinkeye, also called conjunctivitis, is like a common cold in the eye. The white of the eye has a clear membrane that can get red and inflamed. It is usually caused by allergies or by a viral or bacterial infection. Like many viral or bacterial infections, pinkeye can be contagious. It may take a few days to a week to heal, but with this natural solution, you can get rid of pinkeye in no time.

Symptoms of pinkeye include redness of the eye, swollen and red eyelids, watery and excessively dripping eyes, burning or itchy eyes, eyes that are crusty or have a pus-like drainage, and a constant feeling that you have something stuck in the eye even though you don't.

For hundreds of years, herbs have been used as medicine. Many herbs have anti-inflammatory, antiviral and antibacterial properties and can help fight fungal infections.

Yield: 2 tea bags

2 bags organic chamomile tea

1 cup (237 ml) distilled hot water

Bring the distilled water to a boil. Dip two bags of chamomile tea into the water and let them steep for 1 minute. Remove the tea bags and allow them to cool to a comfortably warm temperature (about 30 seconds) and place one tea bag onto each eye. Let them sit for 10–15 minutes. Do not use the same tea bag for both eyes: pinkeye can transfer from one eye to the other. Repeat 2–3 times a day until it clears up.

SAFETY NOTES ...

Be sure to check with your doctor before trying this or any natural remedy.

If you are still experiencing discomfort after a few days of treatment, or if the pinkeye gets worse, seek medical attention.

EXCESS WAX REMOVAL FROM EARS

Many people think that earwax is a bad thing. Actually, it protects the ear, and when at all possible should be left alone. Some individuals create too much earwax, however, so removal can be necessary. Never stick any objects in your ears because they can damage the ear and cause further blockage. The goal is to soften the earwax so that it can exit easily on its own.

Yield: ⅛ cup (30 ml)

1 tbsp (15 ml) warm water

1 tbsp (15 ml) 3% food-grade hydrogen peroxide

Combine the warm water and hydrogen peroxide in a small bowl. Tilt your head, and with a sterile dropper, place 2–4 drops into one ear. Leave the solution in the ear for 5 minutes and then tilt the head in the other direction to drain the solution out. The solution will come out with some excess wax.

Use a cotton ball to remove any wax that has softened on the outer ear. Repeat with the other ear. Do this 2 times a day for up to a week.

SAFETY NOTE...

Never put any foreign objects into an ear such as a toothpick, cotton swab or finger. They can permanently damage your ear. If you experience any pain or discomfort, or if there is a discharge coming out of the ear, seek medical attention.

SWIMMER'S EAR

When it's time to pull out your swimsuit and head into the water for summer fun, the last thing you want to deal with is a sore ear! Sometimes what follows is an ear infection; or more specifically, swimmer's ear. Swimmer's ear is a bacterial infection of the skin on the outer ear canal that often flares up from swimming or from the ear being too wet for a prolonged period of time.

Yield: 2 tsp (10 ml)

1 tsp (5 ml) distilled white vinegar

1 tsp (5 ml) 91% rubbing alcohol

In a small container, combine the vinegar and rubbing alcohol. With a sterile dropper, place a few drops into the ear that is hurting. Leave this solution in the ear for 5 minutes and then drain it out.

The alcohol will help dry up the water in the ear, and the vinegar has antibacterial properties to help with the infection. If at any time the infection worsens, it may be best to seek out your physician for further evaluation.

EXTRA TIP . . .

If you are prone to this type of infection, use this mixture each time you come out of the water. Simply put a few drops in, allow the drops to stay in for a few seconds and then drain.

GINGIVITIS

Gingivitis is gum inflammation in which the gums are usually swollen, red and irritated. If the gums are not properly taken care of, they may show more serious problems. Take care of your teeth by brushing at least twice a day, once in the morning and once in the evening. Always floss your teeth. Follow up with a dental visit for a cleaning every 6 months.

Yield: 1 tbsp (14 g)

1 tbsp (14 g) coconut oil

Before brushing your teeth in the morning, place the coconut oil in your mouth and swish it around. Do this for 15 minutes.

After 15 minutes, spit out the coconut oil into a trash can. It is best not to spit in the sink because the coconut oil can harden and cause plumbing issues. Do not swallow the coconut oil. Rinse your mouth with warm water and brush as usual. Repeat this every morning.

This is called oil pulling. This helps strengthen the gums, aids in removing unwanted bacteria and helps reduce plaque that often builds up on teeth.

Salt can also help with getting rid of gingivitis. Add ½ teaspoon of salt to a tablespoon (15 ml) of water and swish around in your mouth for about a minute. Spit out. Do this twice a day, once in the morning and once in the evening. Continue until the swelling reduces.

One of the best ways to remove inflammation is with ground turmeric. Combine turmeric powder with a little water to make a thick paste. Spread on swollen gums and allow to sit for 10 minutes. Rinse and repeat daily for a few weeks or until the swelling starts to reduce.

Aloe vera has antibacterial properties that can help aid in treating gingivitis. Filet an aloe leaf open and remove the gel inside. Rub on the gums and leave on for 5–10 minutes. Rinse the mouth with cold water. Repeat twice a day until the swelling subsides.

TOOTHACHE RELIEF

There are home remedies that can help temporarily reduce the pain of an aching tooth. It is very important to follow up with your dentist to find the cause of the pain. For short-term relief, try a few of the following options.

CLOVE OIL

Clove oil has a numbing effect. Eugenol is a natural anesthetic that is found in cloves. Place a drop or two of clove oil onto a cotton swab and put it on the tooth that hurts. Leave on for a few minutes and then remove.

PEPPERMINT TEA

Peppermint also has numbing qualities. Dip a peppermint tea bag into hot water and allow it to cool. Place the tea bag on the throbbing tooth. Leave on for 5 minutes. If you want a cooling effect, place the cooled tea bag in the freezer and allow it to freeze for 30 minutes. Place on the tooth for 5–10 minutes.

SALT

Salt can help remove bacteria that may be causing inflammation and pain. Add a teaspoon of salt to a tablespoon (15 ml) of water and swish it around in the mouth for 2–3 minutes, then spit it out. Repeat several times a day.

GROUND TURMERIC

Ground turmeric has antibacterial and antiseptic properties. It can also be used to help reduce pain from a toothache. Create a thick paste with turmeric powder and water and place on the gums and the affected tooth. Leave the paste on for 10 minutes and then rinse off. Turmeric is safe to swallow and can be beneficial in many other ways.

COLLOIDAL SILVER

Colloidal silver is wonderful for dental health. It can help reverse gum disease, reduce plaque buildup and stop tooth pain almost immediately. You can find colloidal silver at any health food store or online. To use, swish some colloidal silver in the mouth for 5 minutes and spit out. Repeat this 2–3 times a day for 2–4 weeks as needed.

WHITENING TEETH

Whitening your teeth can be tricky, especially if you are using store-bought whiteners. I highly encourage people to stay away from these whitening products, as they can be very harmful to your teeth, not to mention that they are super expensive. Here is a natural solution using ingredients you probably already have in your home.

Yield: ½ tsp

1 tsp (2.5 g) ground turmeric

Water to create a paste

Add the ground turmeric to a small bowl and add enough water to create a thick paste. Brush the mixture onto the teeth and let it sit for 5 minutes. Rinse completely and brush your teeth with toothpaste as you normally would. Repeat once a week or until you get the degree of whiteness you are looking for.

Several other ways to brighten your teeth naturally are using the remineralizing toothpaste (see solution on page 118) and bad breath control and mouthwash (see solution on page 119). Both of these solutions have calcium carbonate powder in them, which is incredibly beneficial for whitening your teeth.

Coconut oil, more specifically oil pulling, has also been known to aid in whitening your teeth. See the solution for gingivitis (page 115) for information on how to oil pull.

You can whiten your teeth with turmeric, coconut oil, baking soda and calcium carbonate. If you have crowns, braces or dentures be sure to ask your dentist before trying this solution.

SAFETY NOTE...

Do not use this or any natural solutions for whitening teeth if you wear braces.

REMINERALIZING PEPPERMINT OR CINNAMON TOOTHPASTE

You may have heard that clay has cleansing qualities. You're probably used to seeing clay in the cosmetic industry, but it has many other uses, too. Did you know that clay can be used to clean your teeth? Even better, clay has essential minerals that help keep your mouth healthy naturally.

Calcium carbonate is another beneficial ingredient for good dental health. Like clay, it helps remineralize the teeth. These few changes can help you on your way to better dental health.

Yield: 1/3 cup (75 g)

2 tbsp (23 g) powdered bentonite clay

1½ tbsp (17 g) calcium carbonate powder

4–5 tbsp (60–74 ml) distilled water

15 drops peppermint or 10 drops cinnamon essential oil

Pinch of salt

Pinch of xylitol or stevia powder (optional)

Place the powdered clay and calcium powder in a non-metal bowl. Add the water and work it in well with a wooden spoon or with your hands. Add another tablespoon (15 ml) of water if needed and work it in. You want a soft, somewhat wet clay.

Stir in the essential oil, salt and xylitol or stevia. Transfer the mixture to a squeezable container.

To use, add a small amount of toothpaste to a toothbrush and brush as usual.

Bentonite clay is often used for facial masks and beauty products, but clay can also be used to naturally clean your mouth and teeth. It is full of minerals and has the ability to remove heavy metals and toxins from the mouth.

SAFETY NOTE . . .

It is best to avoid using metal when working with clay, since clay absorbs metals and will become less effective. Don't use metal spoons or bowls and don't store your clay products in metal containers.

BAD BREATH CONTROL AND MOUTHWASH

Mouthwash isn't just for making your breath smell good; it's also for eliminating bacteria, healing gum disease and remineralizing teeth. It can also fight cavities, get rid of unwanted bacteria in the mouth, reduce plaque buildup and keep your teeth clean.

Did you know that calcium carbonate powder can help remineralize your teeth? How about colloidal silver? Colloidal silver has antibacterial properties that help fight off infections, reduce plaque and aid in healing gums. Here is a solution that tastes amazing and is great for your oral health.

Yield: about 2 cups (473 ml)

2 tsp (8 g) calcium carbonate powder

1 oz (30 ml) colloidal silver

1¾ cups (414 ml) distilled water

¼ cup (60 ml) vodka

25 drops peppermint or spearmint essential oil

Place all the ingredients in a glass bottle or jar. Cover and shake to combine. Swish a small amount, about a tablespoon (11 g), in your mouth for 30–60 seconds, then spit it out. Can be used 2–3 times a day.

CANKER SORES

Canker sores are small ulcers or lesions located in the mouth, usually along the baseline of the gums. They hurt! Because the mouth is always wet, healing canker sores can be somewhat challenging.

Common symptoms of canker sores are a tingling or burning sensation that appears 24 hours before the canker sore; white to yellow craters inside the mouth with a red border; and painful sores. You might also experience these less-common symptoms: fever, swollen lymph nodes and feeling run-down or sluggish.

Canker sores are not contagious, and they usually go away on their own within 1–2 weeks. The good news is that you can get rid of the pain that a canker sore causes in a matter of a few hours with only one ingredient: alum powder.

Alum powder is used for making pickles. It pulls water out of the cucumber. It does the same for a canker sore. When you remove the moisture, the ulcer has a chance to heal.

Yield: about a pea size

Alum powder, about the size of a pea

Place a small amount of alum directly onto the canker sore. Allow it to sit on the canker sore for 60 seconds. It is quite bitter, and it can burn slightly. Do not swallow the alum.

After 60 seconds spit out your saliva and the alum. DO NOT RINSE YOUR MOUTH WITH WATER! Within several minutes to 24 hours, the pain will disappear.

The ulcer may stay for a day or two after you treat the canker sore, but the pain will be gone. If the pain is not gone after 24 hours, reapply the alum, repeating the steps above.

SAFETY NOTE ...

Contact your doctor or dentist if canker sores last more than 3 weeks, if you have a fever or if they start to spread throughout your mouth.

COLD SORES

A cold sore is the herpes simplex virus. It creates tiny blisters on or around the mouth, specifically the lips. These blisters break open, ooze and drain. You should not scratch the blisters; this could cause them to spread. Herpes is contagious and can spread to other parts of the body and to other individuals if one is not careful.

An outbreak is usually triggered by a weakened immune system, a poor diet, stress or by simply being run down. Consider making some lifestyle changes that support your immune system.

HERE ARE STEPS TO HELP YOU GET RID OF COLD SORES FAST!

Consider taking a lysine supplement during an outbreak. Lysine can help get rid of cold sores fast. Foods that are high in lysine are meats, dairy, yogurt and cheese.

Apply ice to the cold sore immediately. In order for a cold sore to thrive it needs a warm environment. By applying ice immediately, or even when you feel a tingle, you might be able to reduce the outbreak or shorten the duration.

Avoid acidic foods. The herpes virus loves a too-acidic body. Avoid touching the blister with anything acidic such as vinegar, tomatoes or citrus.

Place 1–2 drops of melaleuca (tea tree oil) on the blister or on the area that is tingling. Spread it with a cotton swab. Repeat 2–3 times a day throughout an outbreak. If using the oil on small children, dilute it with a carrier oil.

Use a lemon balm cream on the blister. Place on the blister 2–3 times a day until it clears up.

Use a healing lip balm (like the one on page 122) to help heal your cold sore.

If you follow these six steps, you can supply your body the healing tools that it needs to help get rid of cold sores quickly.

HEALING LIP BALM

Sometimes, especially in the colder months, lips can crack and become chapped and painful. Here is a healing lip balm to help soothe your lips.

Yield: 3–4 lip balms

2 tsp (10 g) beeswax pellets or grated beeswax

1 tsp (5 g) coconut oil

1 tsp (5 ml) almond oil

2–3 drops of essential oils

Place the beeswax, coconut oil and almond oil in a glass mason jar or a metal bowl. Place the jar or bowl in a double boiler and melt the ingredients.

Once they've melted, remove them from the heat and add the essential oils of your choice. Pour it into lip balm containers and allow it to cool until completely solid (about an hour). This recipe makes 3–4 lip balms, depending on the size of the container you use.

Homemade lip balm is one of the simplest things to make and takes only several minutes to whip up. Use it to heal your cracked lips, get rid of cold sores faster or to soften and smooth your lips.

HEALING ESSENTIAL OILS FOR THE LIPS:

Relieves chapped lips: Add 2 drops of frankincense and 1 drop of lavender.

Fights cold sores: Add 1 drops of melaleuca (tea tree oil) and 2 drops of lemon balm (also known as melissa) essential oil.

Soothes lips: Add 2–3 drops of peppermint.

ALLERGIES

Allergies are a sign of a hypersensitive immune system that reacts to foreign substances such as pet dander or pollen. They can be especially troublesome in the spring, when buds form on trees and pollen starts to spread.

Many people think that coping with allergies means staying indoors or taking medications. There are safer and more effective ways to conquer allergies. Natural herbs have incredible healing properties. One of the herbs that can help eliminate allergies once and for all is nettle leaf, a natural antihistamine. Here are several ways you can use nettle leaf to fight allergies.

Nettle leaf capsules work best for allergies. They can be found in health food stores or online.

Yield: capsules: 1–2, tea: 1 cup (237 ml)

1–2 nettle leaf capsules

1 cup (237 ml) water

1 tea bag of nettle leaf tea

1 tsp (5 ml) raw local honey

1 slice of lemon

2–4 fresh peppermint leaves (or you can add a bag of peppermint tea)

Take 1 nettle leaf capsule 1–2 times a day.

A few other items that can help ease allergies are raw honey, lemon and peppermint. Here is a healing drink that can help with allergies. Organic nettle leaf tea can be found in health food stores or online.

Bring water to a boil. Pour it into a mug and add your nettle leaf tea bag. Steep the tea for 15 minutes. Remove the tea bag and add the honey, lemon and fresh peppermint. You can also pour this over ice for a cold drink. Drink 2–3 glasses of tea a day to help fight allergies.

Consider changing your diet to strengthen your immune system. Try taking a quality probiotic: it can dramatically help reduce allergies, especially during allergy season.

FOAMING FACE WASH AND TONER

For years I have been searching for a face wash that doesn't dry my skin, doesn't make it too oily and isn't made with toxic chemicals. Guess what? It doesn't exist at an affordable price unless it's homemade!

With a few key ingredients, you can make an effective face wash that is nourishing for your skin.

Yield: 1½ cups (355 ml)

1 cup (237 ml) distilled water

¼ cup (60 ml) unscented pure castile liquid soap

2 tbsp (30 ml) liquid coconut oil

1 tbsp (15 ml) pure aloe vera

1 tsp (5 ml) vitamin E oil

15 drops sandalwood essential oil

25 drops geranium essential oil

Place the water, liquid castile soap, coconut oil, aloe vera and vitamin E into a foaming soap dispenser. Swish around to blend slightly. Add in 15 drops of sandalwood essential oil and 25 drops of geranium essential oil.

Before each use, swish to blend. Wash your face using one full pump.

DID YOU KNOW...

Aloe vera is incredibly beneficial for the skin and is an effective toner for all skin types.

The fatty acids in coconut oil can be incredibly beneficial for your skin, including protecting your skin against acne.

Geranium is great for dry skin and sensitive skin. It helps fight acne and is an antibacterial and anti-inflammatory oil that is refreshing and relaxing.

Sandalwood naturally softens the skin, leaving it smooth and silky, and it offers relief for oily skin. It evens out skin that's both dry and oily to create a soft and natural glow.

Foaming face wash evenly covers your skin to remove unwanted dirt and oil. Aloe vera helps tone your skin naturally and leaves your skin soft and vibrant.

ACNE CONTROL MASK

There is no need for expensive prescription creams or soaps for coping with acne; you just need a few natural ingredients that really make a difference.

Zinc is extremely valuable for getting rid of acne. Being deficient in zinc can often lead to an acne breakout. Consider supplementing your diet with zinc. Putting a paste of zinc powder and water on current pimples should help them heal quickly.

Consider cleaning up your diet by reducing processed foods. One of the best things you can do to help prevent acne is drink 16 ounces (473 ml) of water with ½ lemon squeezed into it first thing in the morning, every morning. Do this on an empty stomach. This will help rid your body of toxins and help stop pimples before they start.

Yield: 2-3 masks

½ banana

½ tsp raw honey

½ tsp olive oil

½ tsp lemon juice

⅛ tsp turmeric

Place all the ingredients in a blender and blend until smooth. Spread the mixture liberally onto a clean face and allow it to sit for 20–30 minutes. Rinse with warm water and blot dry. This should make enough for several uses, so store the remaining solution in the refrigerator for up to a week. Repeat this mask 2–3 times a week for best results.

EXTRA TIP...

If the turmeric leaves a yellowish hue on your face, mix together ¼ cup (60 ml) of warm water with 1 tablespoon (15 ml) apple cider vinegar. Dip a cotton ball into the solution and wipe onto your clean face. The yellow tint should come right off.

DID YOU KNOW...

Bananas can help fade dark spots and even out your skin tone. They can aid in reducing dryness, moisturizing the skin and preventing aging.

Turmeric is a natural anti-inflammatory with antibacterial properties. It can help get rid of the bacteria that promote pimples.

Honey is an incredible moisturizer that doesn't leave an oily residue. It also helps prevent acne with its antibacterial properties.

Lemon juice has citric acid, which helps reduce blemishes and evens out skin tone.

CHEST, THROAT AND IMMUNE SYSTEM

It can be hard to find a natural remedy for a sore throat, stuffy nose, stomachache or the flu. In this chapter, we explore how you can get rid of the flu up to three times faster than usual just by taking one supplement (page 132). Learn how to ease a sore throat with a few simple ingredients (page 129). Did you know that you can clear your stuffy nose, caused by allergies or a common cold, with yes, three—simple ingredients (page 128)? We can even make a vapor rub for those times when we need a little more support to help clear the nasal passages (page 130).

Do you often get heartburn or acid reflux, or do you suffer from GERD? Learn how to treat all three of these ailments with a variety of natural solutions (page 133).

Are you looking for a safe way to restore your electrolytes? Electrolytes often need replenishing after a good exercise session, after illness and during heat waves or dehydration. We've been told for years to replenish electrolytes with a sugary drink, but there are better options. Pure coconut water and freshly juiced celery are two of the best ways that you can replenish your electrolytes (page 135).

If you are looking for solutions that are simple, effective and easy to make, you've selected the right chapter. You might be surprised how many ingredients you already have in your home for treating your ailments naturally.

NASAL DECONGESTANT RINSE

When you can't breathe out of your nose, it can be hard to carry on with everyday tasks. A simple saline rinse can really help you clear your nasal passages.

Purchase a good neti pot or nasal bulb to use this solution. This will help you remove any excess mucus from your sinuses. It can also help with removing dust, pollen and other pollutants from the nasal passages. The neti pot and the bulb are inexpensive and will last many years.

Most nasal rinses consist of a simple saline solution. One way to enhance them is to add colloidal silver. Did you know that colloidal silver was used for many years as a natural antibiotic? According to Dr. Harry Margraph, a biochemist and silver researcher, "Silver is the best all-around germ fighter we have."

Yield: about 1 cup (237 ml)

1 cup (237 ml) distilled water

¼ tsp non-iodized salt

1 tbsp (15 ml) colloidal silver

Bring the distilled water to a slight boil in a small saucepan. Add the non-iodized salt and stir until dissolved. Allow the mixture to cool. Stir in the colloidal silver. Pour half of the liquid into a nasal bulb or neti pot. Tilt your head to the side and gently pour the liquid into one nostril; let the solution pour through the other nostril. Pour the other half of the solution into the neti pot or nasal bulb and repeat with the other nostril.

COUGH AND SORE THROAT SYRUP

Having a cough and sore throat can be such a nuisance. Thankfully, with three simple ingredients, you can have a homemade cough and sore throat syrup on hand for those times when you need something that really works.

Yield: about ½ cup (118 ml)

3 tbsp (45 ml) fresh lemon juice

3 tbsp (45 ml) raw honey

3 tbsp (45 ml) food-grade vegetable glycerin

In a medium bowl, freshly squeeze 1 lemon for 3 tablespoons (45 ml) of juice. Pour in the honey and food-grade vegetable glycerin and stir well. Place in a flip-top bottle or mason jar. Seal tightly and store in the refrigerator for up to a month. Make this solution in small doses and only when you need it.

To use, take 1–2 teaspoons (21–43 ml) every 4 hours.

Vegetable glycerin is a sweet, thick liquid made from plant oils. Its thick nature easily coats the back of a sore throat and creates a syrup consistency one expects from a cough and sore throat remedy.

SAFETY NOTE...

This syrup is only for children older than 1 year of age and for adults.

DID YOU KNOW...

Raw or local honey offers antibacterial activity that can help heal common ailments like coughs and sore throats?

Food-grade glycerin is incredible for coating the throat. It relieves that scratchy feeling when you aren't feeling your best.

Lemon is loaded with vitamin C and can aid in boosting your immune system.

VAPOR RUB

When you aren't feeling well, whether from the flu or a common cold, pull out this vapor rub and it will help you feel better fast. Rub a little on your chest to open up your airways or put a little under your nose as an intense healing tool.

There are several other ways you can use this vapor rub. Did you know that eucalyptus, peppermint and rosemary all can help repel mosquitoes? Spread a little on your skin before heading outdoors and watch those bugs take off! Have a headache? Rub a little of this vapor rub onto your temples and the back of your neck and the pain will disappear in no time.

Yield: ½ cup (115 g)

1 tbsp (14 g) beeswax pellets

½ cup (109 g) solid coconut oil

½ tsp vitamin E oil

45 drops eucalyptus essential oil

15 drops peppermint essential oil

10 drops rosemary essential oil

In a medium bowl, melt the beeswax and coconut oil over a double boiler. Once they're melted, remove the bowl from the heat and add the vitamin E oil and essential oils. Pour it immediately into a container and allow it to cool completely. The mixture will thicken as it cools.

Store it in a cool dry place. It will last for up to a year.

When congested, place a small amount on the chest and rub in. You can also rub it under your nose to help clear your sinuses.

FLU

Getting the flu can put you out of commission for upwards of a week. Did you know that there is a natural remedy that can actually help you get rid of the flu up to three times faster? This natural solution is black elderberry syrup, also called black elderberry extract.

Black elderberry syrup can help combat colds, sinus infections and common flu symptoms. It can help build your immune system and is high in antioxidants.

Yield: 2 cups (473 ml)

1 cup (165 g) dried black elderberries

1 cinnamon stick

2 cups (473 ml) filtered water

1 cup (237 ml) local honey

Add the dried black elderberries, cinnamon stick and water to a small saucepan. Bring to a boil and then reduce heat and simmer uncovered. Simmer for 20 minutes or until the liquid reduces by half. Strain the syrup into a pint mason jar, pressing down on the berries to remove all the syrup. Discard the elderberries. Allow the syrup to fully cool (it will produce about 1 cup [237 ml]). Once cool, add the honey to the syrup and stir well. Store in the refrigerator for up to 6–8 months. At the first sign of the flu, take ½ tablespoon (7 ml) to 1 tablespoon (15 ml) every 2–3 hours for adults, and children can take ½ teaspoon to 1 teaspoon every 2–3 hours. Take it until the flu symptoms disappear.

Elderberries can help get rid of the flu up to three times faster! You don't need fresh elderberries, dried elderberries are just as effective and can easily be found at health stores or online.

HEARTBURN, ACID REFLUX AND GERD

Heartburn, acid reflux and GERD can occur together or separately. For mild cases, you can most likely find relief in a natural solution. Every person is different, so try these three solutions and see which works best for you.

There are three common ingredients that you most likely already have in your kitchen that can help relieve your symptoms.

Yield: apple cider water: 1 cup (237 ml), baking soda water: 1 cup (237 ml), calcium carbonate juice : 1 cup (237 ml)

APPLE CIDER WATER

1–3 tsp (5–15 ml) raw apple cider vinegar

8 oz (237 ml) water

BAKING SODA WATER

½ tsp baking soda

8 oz (237 ml) water

CALCIUM CARBONATE JUICE

½ tsp calcium carbonate powder

8 oz (237 ml) citric juice or water

SAFETY NOTE . . .

Talk to a qualified healthcare provider before trying any of these remedies and to discuss your options.

APPLE CIDER WATER

Sometimes you have too little acid in your stomach, which can cause multiple problems. Apple cider vinegar adds acid back into your stomach and can naturally help eliminate symptoms.

Drink 1 teaspoon (5 ml) of raw apple cider vinegar mixed into water. Repeat up to 2 times a day to help relieve symptoms. If you still have noticeable symptoms, increase the raw apple cider vinegar 1 teaspoon (5 ml) at a time (not to exceed 3 teaspoons [15 ml]).

BAKING SODA WATER

Baking soda helps neutralize stomach acid and reduces the burning sensation you can often feel.

Mix ½ teaspoon of baking soda into water and drink. Do not exceed more than ½ teaspoon in a 24-hour period and do not use this method for more than 1 week.

CALCIUM CARBONATE JUICE

Calcium carbonate powder is the active ingredient in antacid tablets. The benefit of using pure calcium carbonate powder is that there are no artificial colors or sweeteners.

Always check the label for dosage information before taking calcium carbonate orally.

Mix a half teaspoon of calcium carbonate powder with juice or water and drink with a meal.

Also consider making some lifestyle changes and try to remove processed foods from your diet. Look into taking some quality digestive enzymes, as they can help considerably.

STOMACHACHE

Stomachaches can have any number of causes. You can use ginger and peppermint several ways to calm the stomach.

Yield: essential oils for stomachaches: 1–2 drops, healing stomachache drink: about 1 cup (237 ml)

ESSENTIAL OILS FOR STOMACHACHES

1–2 drops of peppermint essential oil

1–2 drops of ginger essential oil

HEALING STOMACHACHE DRINK

1-inch (25-mm) cube fresh ginger, peeled and sliced

2–3 sprigs fresh peppermint or 1 bag peppermint tea

8 oz (237 ml) boiling water

2 tsp (10 ml) raw honey

Ginger and peppermint naturally calms an upset stomach, helps the digestive system break down heavy foods and can ease motion and morning sickness.

ESSENTIAL OILS FOR STOMACHACHES

If you have ginger or peppermint essential oils, or both, they can help relieve stomachaches in several ways.

First, try inhaling or smelling them. Sometimes the smell alone can help relieve a stomachache.

Next, try rubbing 1–2 drops of either oil onto your stomach. Depending on the quality of your oils, you may need to dilute them with a carrier oil (like coconut, olive oil, jojoba oil or almond oil). Always dilute peppermint and ginger essential oils with a carrier oil for use on children. Finally, try adding 3–4 drops of either of these oils to a diffuser.

HEALING STOMACHACHE DRINK

If you don't have essential oils, try this healing drink that you can make with ingredients you probably have in your kitchen.

Put the ginger and fresh mint into a large mug. Pour boiling water into the cup and allow it to steep for 15 minutes. Stir in the raw honey until it dissolves completely. Strain and drink hot, or strain and pour over a glass of ice for a cold beverage.

SAFETY NOTE . . .

Omit the raw honey for children under the age of one.

RESTORING ELECTROLYTES

Electrolytes are critical for a healthy functioning body. You can quickly lose electrolytes from exercise, illness, dehydration and even from a heat wave.

The major electrolytes include calcium, bicarbonate, sodium, magnesium, chloride, phosphate and potassium. When your body becomes deficient in these, it is imperative that you replenish them. Do not turn to common sugar sport drinks that are marketed to young kids and adults. Turn to quality, wholesome foods! Here are two of the best ways that you can replenish your electrolytes naturally.

Yield: 14–16 oz (414–473 ml)

CELERY JUICE

1 head of celery, organic if possible

COCONUT WATER

1 fresh, young, green coconut (young coconuts produce a sweeter drink)

CELERY JUICE

Cut up the celery into 4-inch (10-cm) pieces. Juice the entire head of celery by running it through a juicer. If you do not have a juicer, you can use a high-powered blender. Blend for about a minute and then strain. One head of celery should yield 14–16 ounces (414–473 ml) of celery juice. It is best to drink it right away.

COCONUT WATER

Run a paring knife under the top part of the coconut and pop it off. Underneath it, in the center, is a soft area. Carefully carve out a hole big enough for a straw to fit in, holding the coconut away from you over a sink to avoid getting squirted. Coconut water stains, so be careful to not get it on your clothing. Drain the water out of the coconut or simply place a straw into it and drink.

EXTRA TIP...

If you cannot get your hands on green coconuts, look for pure coconut water that is not made from concentrate and does not have added ingredients or preservatives.

HANDS, LEGS, ARMS AND FEET

From a foaming hand wash to a natural sunscreen, this chapter is filled with remedies that everyone will use.

Have you ever wanted to make a foaming hand soap that wasn't full of chemicals and was super cost-effective? You can learn how in this chapter on page 138. How about a hand sanitizer? Often hand sanitizers are loaded with alcohol and can be very drying to your skin. Learn how to make an effective hand sanitizer that will actually soften your hands (page 139)!

Let's talk about body wash for a minute. Have you seen the ingredients of a store-bought body wash? Yikes! Body wash is simple to make and can be enhanced with some of your favorite natural scents (page 138).

Finding a deodorant that works and doesn't have aluminum or other toxic ingredients has been a challenge for many years. I share two terrific natural deodorant solutions in this chapter that work incredibly well (page 140 and page 141).

Have you been on the lookout for a natural sunscreen? Sunscreen is expensive, but it doesn't have to be. With only a few minutes of your time, you can make a natural sunscreen that the whole family can use (page 143).

So whether you are looking to get rid of smelly feet or relieve sore muscles or achy joints, there are plenty of helpful ways to treat common problems of the hands, legs, arms and feet.

FOAMING HAND WASH

Foaming hand soap can be expensive. You can make your own for a fraction of the price of store-bought. You will need to recycle an old foaming soap pump dispenser or purchase a new one.

You can easily make a scented foaming hand wash with essential oils but, if you'd like, you can skip the essential oils and just buy some scented castile liquid soap. Here is how easy it is to make your own foaming hand wash.

Yield: 1¼ cups (296 ml)

1 cup (237 ml) distilled or filtered water

¼ cup (60 ml) castile liquid soap (scented or unscented)

20–30 drops favorite essential oils (optional)

Place the water and castile soap in the foaming soap dispenser. Swish around to blend slightly.

Add essential oils of choice.

Swish to blend. Use 1 pump to wash your hands.

SENSITIVE SKIN BODY WASH

Have you ever looked at the ingredients of your favorite body wash? I would take an educated guess that you might not recognize a few of them. What's even worse is that a lot of these ingredients are toxic.

Making your own body wash is simple and takes only minutes. Do not add essential oils to it because they can affect its thickness. If you want a scented body wash, consider grating a natural soap bar that is scented with wholesome ingredients.

Yield: about 1½ cups (355 ml)

1½ cups (355 ml) distilled boiling water

1 tbsp (5 g) soap flakes or grated natural soap bar

Heat the water to a boil. Remove from heat and stir in the soap flakes. Stir until dissolved. Allow to cool and set for 24 hours; it will gel as it sits. Pour into a squeezable container. Gently shake before each use.

To use, place about a quarter-sized amount onto a washcloth or loofah. Wash as you normally would.

HAND SANITIZER

Getting germs off your hands or those of your little ones can be a priority, especially during cold and flu season. The best way is by using soap and warm water, of course. If you are unable to wash your hands, a hand sanitizer makes a great alternative. If children are using this sanitizer, use witch hazel instead of vodka.

Yield: about ½ cup (118 ml)

½ cup (118 ml) pure aloe vera gel

1 tbsp (15 ml) witch hazel or vodka

5 drops sage or tea tree essential oil (optional)

10 drops lavender essential oil (optional)

In a bowl, combine the aloe vera gel, witch hazel or vodka and essential oil. Stir until well mixed. Transfer to a squeezable small container. To use, place about a dime-sized amount onto your hands and rub them together.

DID YOU KNOW...

Some essential oils can fight off germs by killing off certain bacteria, viruses and fungi. Germ-fighting essential oils are lemon, sage, tea tree oil, clove, thyme, lemongrass, cinnamon, pine and eucalyptus.

Aloe vera gel has antibacterial and antifungal properties. It softens the hands naturally and can help dilute the essential oils in this solution.

Witch hazel or vodka paired with the essential oils helps kill germs for an incredibly effective hand sanitizer.

Essential oils, alcohol, witch hazel and aloe vera all help get rid of unwanted germs on your hands. Separately, these ingredients work very well, but combine them together and you create a powerful germ-fighting hand sanitizer.

EASY DEODORANT SPRAY

Have you been searching for an all-natural deodorant recipe that actually works? Most store-bought deodorants are toxic and should be avoided if possible. Here is an incredibly simple solution that works every time.

Yield: about ⅓ cup (78 ml)

2 tsp (10 ml) distilled white vinegar

¼ cup (60 ml) ethanol alcohol (vodka or gin works best)

Essential oils (optional)

SCALE FOR SPECIFIC PROTECTION (TO GET THE PROOF, DOUBLE THE % ALCOHOL PER VOLUME)

70–90 proof = light coverage

90–120 proof = medium coverage

120+ proof = strong coverage

In a fine mist 2-ounce (60 ml) sprayer, add the distilled vinegar, ethanol alcohol of choice and essential oils, if using, and shake well.

Apply 2 spritzes to each underarm. Allow to dry slightly (about a minute) before putting on clothes.

When transitioning to a natural deodorant you might have an adjustment period. Don't worry; after 3 days your underarm will adjust.

FOLLOW THIS SCHEDULE

On the first day, spray 2–3 spritzes on each underarm, in the morning and then again around 3 p.m. On the second day, spray 2 spritzes on each underarm in the morning and then again right before bed. On the third day, spray 2–3 spritzes on each underarm for all-day coverage.

SAFTEY NOTES . . .

Ethanol alcohol and rubbing alcohol are not the same thing. Rubbing alcohol can irritate the skin, eyes, mucous membranes and upper respiratory tract.

Do not use this deodorant on children unless you switch out the alcohol out for witch hazel.

SENSITIVE SKIN DEODORANT CREAM

It is hard to find a deodorant that doesn't contain toxic ingredients. When transitioning to a natural solution for your armpits, you may find that even some natural ingredients irritate the skin. Baking soda, especially, can be used in too large a quantity and can cause your skin to break out. The solution below is very nourishing for the skin, and it uses the appropriate amounts so your skin won't be irritated.

Yield: 2 oz (60 g)

2 tbsp (30 g) shea butter

1 tbsp (15 g) mango butter

1 tbsp (14 g) coconut oil

1 tbsp (9 g) tapioca flour

1 tbsp (14 g) arrowroot powder

1½ tsp (6.5 g) baking soda

15–20 drops of essential oils of choice (optional)

In a double boiler, melt the shea butter and mango butter. While the butters are melting, add the coconut oil to a small glass or metal bowl. Add the tapioca flour, arrowroot powder and baking soda to the coconut oil and work them in with the back of a metal soup spoon.

Add the melted butters to the coconut oil mixture and stir until well combined. Place the bowl in the refrigerator for 15–20 minutes. Remove it from the refrigerator and scrape the hardened sides to the center of the bowl. Add the essential oils, if you desire. Using the whisk attachment of an electric mixture, whip for about a minute or until the mixture has a creamy texture. Pour or spoon into a 2-ounce (60-ml) container and allow to fully set for 2–4 hours.

Rub a pea-sized amount onto the underarms with your fingers. Allow the deodorant to absorb into the skin for a few minutes before putting on your clothes.

Shea butter is used often in natural beauty products, and for good reasons. It moisturizes, reduces inflammation and smooths the skin. One benefit shea butter offers in this solution is that it may slow down hair growth of the underarm, which allows women to shave less.

DID YOU KNOW...

When transitioning to a natural deodorant you may have an adjustment period. Natural deodorants are designed to allow your body to sweat. Sweat is your body's natural mechanism for releasing toxins and cooling off. Your body will adjust to this new deodorant. In a short period of time, the wetness will reduce and in some cases completely disappear.

CREAMY LOTION

Have you ever made a lotion at home only to find that you are left with an incredibly greasy final product? Most lotions are made of oils, but it is very important that the lotion be emulsified properly. This solution shows you how to effectively emulsify water and oils together. It might take a little effort, but the end results are fantastic!

Yield: 8 oz (227 g)

½ cup (118 ml) sweet almond oil

2 tbsp (30 g) beeswax pellets

1 tsp (5 ml) vitamin E oil

²/₃ cup (156 ml) room temperature distilled water

Essential oils (optional)

Add the sweet almond oil and beeswax to a double boiler and heat until fully melted. Remove from the heat and stir in the vitamin E. In a blender, add the distilled water. Turn the blender on to medium speed and add the oil and beeswax mixture in a slow and steady stream, sometimes drop by drop. Do it as slowly as possible; this process should take 5–7 minutes. If you go too quickly, the oil and water will not emulsify. When you're done, the lotion will have a creamy texture. If there is a little water left, drain it off.

Spoon the lotion into an 8-ounce (237-ml) glass jar, preferably with a wide mouth. Stir in essential oils if desired. Make this lotion in small batches. Vitamin E acts as a natural preservative so the shelf life is about 3 months.

You can make a creamy lotion by emulsifying water and oil together. This isn't hard to accomplish, but it does require some patience. A slow and steady stream is the key to a successful lotion.

SUNSCREEN

We all need the sun in our lives. Since it's one of the most healing sources of energy on the planet, it's important to gradually work sunlight into your life. Start out by being in the sun 15 minutes a day and gradually work up to a half hour. You will be able to tolerate the sun more as you increase your time.

When you plan on being in the sun for hours upon hours, it is important to protect your skin from overexposure. Most sunscreens on the market are loaded with toxic ingredients. It is so simple to make your own at home, and it's much more cost-effective.

Yield: 8 oz (227 g)

½ cup (118 ml) coconut or avocado oil

2 tbsp (28 g) beeswax

1 tsp (5 ml) vitamin E oil

⅔ cup (156 ml) warm distilled water

2 tbsp (23 g) non-nano zinc oxide powder

In a double boiler, add the coconut oil and beeswax and heat until fully melted. Remove from the heat and stir in the vitamin E. In a blender, add the warm distilled water. Turn the blender on to medium speed and add in the oil and beeswax mixture in a slow and steady stream, sometimes drop by drop. Do this as slowly as possible; the process should take 5–7 minutes. If you go too quickly, the oil and water will not emulsify. Once you're done, the lotion will have a creamy texture. If there is water left over, drain it off.

Spoon the lotion into a medium-sized bowl and stir in 2 tablespoons (23 g) of zinc oxide powder. Zinc oxide is a very fine powder, so it is best to use a mask to avoid breathing it in. Whisk until well combined. Spoon into an 8-ounce (237-ml) glass jar, preferably with a wide mouth. Make this sunscreen in small batches. Vitamin E acts as a natural preservative so the shelf life is 3–6 months.

To use, spread it evenly onto your skin. A little goes a long way. It will have a white hue; this is normal. This solution has about a 15 SPF. Apply again after swimming or sweating. Reapply every 1½–2 hours or as needed.

This is not a sunblock. It is best to stay out of the sun during the peak hours of 11 a.m.–4 p.m. If you are enjoying the sun during peak times, shade yourself with an umbrella, a large brimmed hat and some loose clothing. Protect your skin with an all-natural sunblock during peak hours.

If you don't want to make your own lotion, add 2 tablespoons (23 g) of non-nano zinc oxide powder to 1 cup (237 ml) of natural lotion and stir until well combined. Apply this as your sunscreen.

FOOT ODOR

Foot odor can happen for a number of different reasons, but proper foot care can help. Try to keep your feet dry. Wear shoes that allow air to circulate around your feet. Always wear clean socks. Wash your shoes if you suspect there might be a fungus growing in them.

Yield: 5 cups (1 L)

½ cup (118 ml) apple cider vinegar

1 quart (946 ml) warm water

½ cup (103 g) baking soda

20 drops tea tree oil

Place the vinegar and warm water in a container large enough for your feet. Soak for 10–15 minutes and then dry your feet. Repeat this 1–2 times a day.

Follow up with a baking soda and tea tree oil powder by mixing the two ingredients into a container with a lid. Gently shake. To use, sprinkle onto your dry feet, between your toes and into your shoes. Repeat this 2–3 times a day.

ATHLETE'S FOOT

Athlete's foot doesn't happen only to athletes; it can happen to anyone. Athlete's foot (*Tinea pedis*) is a fungal infection of the foot. It often shows up between the toes and under the toenails if the conditions are right. Athlete's foot thrives in damp conditions and can cause rash-like symptoms. The infection can spread to the hands, nails and groin. It is important to treat athlete's foot for 3–4 weeks to prevent spreading. Here is a three-step solution to help you get rid of athlete's foot quickly.

Yield: varies

STEP 1

Warm water

½ cup (118 ml) apple cider vinegar

3 tbsp (45 g) salt

STEP 2

3 drops tea tree oil

1 tsp (5 g) coconut oil

STEP 3

Colloidal silver

STEP 1

Find a bucket or container large enough for your feet to fit in. Fill it with enough warm water to fully submerge your feet. Add the apple cider vinegar and salt, stirring to dissolve. Soak your feet for 20 minutes in this solution. Remove your feet and fully dry them.

STEP 2

Mix the tea tree oil with coconut oil. Rub it into your feet, not forgetting to get between your toes. Allow this mixture to fully absorb into the skin.

STEP 3

Place some colloidal silver in a spray bottle. Right before bed, spray your feet with colloidal silver and rub it in. Allow it to fully dry.

JOCK ITCH

Jock itch, also called *tinea cruris*, has rash-like symptoms and causes redness or irritation of the groin area, inner thighs and/or the buttocks. It is a fungal and sometimes bacterial infection that doesn't only itch, but can cause a burning sensation. It can be contagious. Here is a two-step process for getting rid of jock itch.

Yield: wet solution: about ⅓ cup (78 ml), dry solution: about ½ cup (90 g)

¼ cup (60 ml) water

1 tbsp (15 ml) white vinegar

½ cup (112 g) arrowroot powder or organic corn starch

15 drops tea tree oil

In a small bowl, add the water and white vinegar. With a cotton pad, gently wipe this solution onto the affected area 2–3 times a day. Allow to fully dry.

In the meantime, place the arrowroot powder in a small container with a lid. Add in the tea tree oil and put the lid on. Gently shake the mixture to infuse the powder with the oils. Sprinkle a small amount onto the affected area as needed.

It is important to continue this process for 3–4 weeks even if your symptoms go away. Jock itch can quickly come back if you don't fully get rid of it. Being proactive can help prevent it from coming back.

SAFETY NOTE ...

If your symptoms become worse at any time, seek medical attention right away. You may need additional medication for a bacterial infection.

DID YOU KNOW...

Jock itch doesn't necessarily come from a jock strap; it can thrive in any moist environment of the groin area.

Jock itch doesn't just affect men; women can get jock itch, too.

Jock itch can spread to other parts of your body, especially your feet. Then it is called athlete's foot.

HEALING BALM (FOR SORE MUSCLES AND JOINT PAIN)

When your muscles and joints are in pain, it can be hard to find something natural and safe for relief. This solution is super easy to make and contains a number of oils that are healing for muscle and joint pain.

Yield: 4 oz (113 g)

3 tbsp (41 g) beeswax pellets

1 tbsp (15 g) shea butter

2 tbsp (27 g) coconut oil

2 tbsp (30 ml) almond oil

15 drops peppermint oil

15 drops eucalyptus oil

15 drops wintergreen oil

5 drops clove oil

5 drops lavender oil

In a double boiler, melt together the beeswax, shea butter, coconut oil and almond oil. Leave it in the double boiler until completely melted, then remove it from the heat and allow it to cool for a few minutes. Add the essential oils and gently stir into the mixture. Transfer this solution to a small glass jar and allow it to fully set for about an hour.

To use, place about a dime-sized amount into your hand and work it into the area that has sore muscles and/or joint pain. This is a very thick and waxy balm. This texture will help penetrate the muscle area. Apply as needed.

Peppermint, eucalyptus and wintergreen essential oils all have a cooling effect on the skin. Clove oil, however, has a warmer effect on the skin and has a natural numbing quality to it.

SKIN IRRITATIONS AND HEALTH CONDITIONS

There are so many skin irritants out there, but what is one to do about them? Treat them naturally, of course! Whether you have a skin disorder from a weakened immune system like eczema, psoriasis or rosacea; or a skin irritant from nature like poison ivy, bug bites or a bee sting, there are plenty of natural remedies to help. Did you know that one of the most healing foods for eczema, psoriasis and rosacea is celery juice? Celery juice helps replenish your hydrochloric acid and is extremely beneficial for treatment of these common conditions.

When the weather gets nice, those pesky insects can be such a nuisance! Gear yourself up with natural ingredients that can help solve common problems caused by insects. Vinegar can help get rid of the sting that a bee causes and aid in getting rid of poison ivy and poison oak. Bentonite clay and calcium carbonate powder can take the itch out of any bug bite fast.

Would you know how to clean a cut or burn properly if an accident happened and you had no first aid items? A few natural ingredients that you probably already have in your home can effectively treat these conditions. Speaking of first aid kits, did you know that many homes don't have a first aid kit? You can start building your own by making a Flexible, Reusable Ice Pack (page 164), a Reusable Heating Pad (page 165) and a do-it-yourself assortment of bandages (page 166). Using natural ingredients for health remedies is actually very simple and cost-effective.

ECZEMA TREATMENT

If you or someone you know suffers from eczema, there may be relief in your near future. Eczema is a skin disorder that inflames the skin, which can create large patches of itchy and flaky skin and blisters on the body.

An eczema breakout is a sign of an overactive immune system that needs support. It is a signal that something isn't right internally and some changes need to be made. Consider exploring the idea that you may have an allergy to a certain food or an environmental contaminant. It might be beneficial to do an elimination diet or to seek out an allergist for allergy testing.

Diet and lifestyle are huge components in treating eczema. Removal of processed foods, wheat and dairy can often help clear it up. Avoid perfumes, dyes and anything with artificial flavors or scents.

One of the best ways to reduce inflammation caused by eczema is with one common food item: celery. The juice from celery has anti-inflammatory properties, which can aid in treating eczema. Drink this juice every morning on an empty stomach to support your immune system.

Yield: juice: 14–16 oz (414–473 ml), lotion: 8 oz (227 g)

1 head of celery, organic if possible

1 batch of Creamy Lotion (page 142)

25 drops lavender essential oil

5 drops tea tree essential oil

2 capsules olive leaf extract

Cut up the celery into 4-inch (10-cm) pieces. Juice the entire head by running the celery through a juicer. If you do not have a juicer, use a high-powered blender for about a minute and then strain. One head of celery should yield 14–16 ounces (414–473 ml) of celery juice. It is best to drink celery juice right away and on an empty stomach.

Here is a simple lotion to help heal the skin from an eczema breakout.

Make a batch of Creamy Lotion. Stir the lavender essential oil, tea tree oil and olive leaf extract into the lotion. Place a small amount onto the infected skin and rub it in. Keep your skin moisturized with this lotion as much as possible. Consider taking olive leaf extract orally to help build your immune system back to good health.

PLAQUE PSORIASIS TREATMENT

Plaque psoriasis is a skin condition that starts underneath the skin. Flare-ups often happen when an overactive immune system causes new skin cells to form. A person without psoriasis produces new skin cells every 28 to 30 days, but someone with psoriasis produces new skin cells at a much faster rate, every 3 to 4 days. The overproduction of skin cells produces a scaly, itchy rash, which often presents in dry patches.

There is no cure for psoriasis, but there are natural treatments. Food is your best form of medicine, and your diet should be analyzed for potential allergies and triggers. Consider eliminating processed foods, wheat, alcohol, dairy, red meat and processed sugars from your diet. Add more healing fruits and vegetables and supplements that support and build your immune system. Live a more "green" and natural lifestyle. Often, environmental circumstances can trigger a psoriasis outbreak. Eliminate harmful chemicals whenever possible, especially in your home.

One of the best foods to support your immune system is celery. Celery juice has anti-inflammatory properties that can reduce inflammation and help with your treatment for psoriasis. Drink this juice every morning on an empty stomach to support your immune system.

CELERY

Cut up the celery into 4-inch (10-cm) pieces. Juice the entire head by running the celery through a juicer. If you do not have a juicer, use a high-powered blender for about a minute and then strain. One head of celery should yield 14–16 ounces (414–473 ml) of celery juice. It is best to drink celery juice right away and on an empty stomach.

TURMERIC (CURCUMIN)

Turmeric is nature's natural immunity booster. Its active ingredient—curcuminoids—is an antioxidant. When taken orally, curcumin can help with the treatment of psoriasis.

500 MG CURCUMIN

Take this once a day, or according to package directions.

SAFETY NOTE . . .

If you are under 18, pregnant or nursing, or if you have a medical condition and/or are taking medications, always speak to a qualified healthcare provider before taking this or any product.

ROSACEA TREATMENT

Rosacea is a common condition that causes inflammation of the skin, such as redness on the face and it often causes adult-like acne. Dilated blood vessels can appear on the face; swelling is often a symptom. In advanced cases, thickening of the skin can be present.

Doctors do not know what causes rosacea, but natural treatments and lifestyle changes can greatly improve it. Consider eliminating hot soups, spicy foods, soy sauce, beans and pods, dairy, chocolate and strongly acidic foods. Alcohol and hot beverages should also be eliminated when possible.

It is best to limit exposure to saunas, hot baths and excessively warm environments. Humidity, extreme cold, strong winds and overexposure to the sun can trigger a flare-up.

The best way to treat rosacea is to build a healthy immune system. Rosacea is more than just a skin problem; it is your skin telling you that something internally needs to be addressed. Cleaning up your diet is imperative when treating rosacea. Consider doing some allergy testing or put yourself on an elimination diet to rule out foods to which you might have an allergy. Remove all processed foods, table sugar and artificial sweeteners, dairy and refined vegetable oils. Fried foods should be avoided entirely.

One of the best foods to support your immune system is celery. Celery juice has anti-inflammatory properties that can reduce inflammation and help with your treatment plan for rosacea. Drink this juice every morning on an empty stomach to support your immune system.

CELERY
Cut up the celery into 4-inch (10-cm) pieces. Juice the entire head by running the celery through a juicer. If you do not have a juicer, use a high-powered blender for about a minute and then strain. One head of celery should yield 14–16 ounces (414–473 ml) of celery juice. It is best to drink celery juice right away and on an empty stomach.

TURMERIC (CURCUMIN)
Turmeric is nature's natural immunity booster. Its active ingredient—curcuminoids—is an antioxidant. When taken orally, curcumin can help with the treatment of rosacea.

500 MG CURCUMIN
Take once or twice daily, according to package directions.

Finally, create a healing gel to help relieve the pain and symptoms that accompanies rosacea (see next page).

DID YOU KNOW ...

Zinc can also benefit people who suffer from rosacea. Consider taking an oral supplement of zinc sulfate and protect your skin from sun exposure with a sunscreen made with zinc oxide (see page 143).

SOOTHING ROSACEA GEL

Yield: ¼ cup (61 g)

¼ cup (85 g) pure aloe vera gel

½ tsp raw honey

2 drops helichrysum essential oil

1 drop chamomile essential oil

In a small container, add the aloe vera gel and the raw honey. Mix well to combine. Pour into a squeeze-top bottle and add the essential oils. Place a small amount into your hand and work the gel into the skin on your face. Apply 2 times a day for best results.

Helichrysum oil has been in use for centuries and it is considered one of the most treasured essential oils on the planet. It helps fight acne, skin inflammation and helps heal wounds. It has antibiotic and anti-fungal healing properties.

MINOR SKIN BURNS

Being in the sun too long, hot liquids, heat, chemicals and steam can all cause minor to severe burns. This solution is for a first-degree burn, which is minor damage to the skin that may include red skin that has not blistered.

Yield: ¹/₃ cup (81 g)

¹/₃ cup (112 g) pure aloe vera gel

8 drops lavender essential oil

½ tsp vitamin E oil

In a small bowl, combine the aloe vera gel, lavender and vitamin E. Stir until combined. Pour into a squeezable container. To use, squeeze a little into the palm of your hand and gently rub on the burn. Repeat as needed.

Vitamin E is a powerful oil that can assist with skin regeneration. To speed up the healing process of a burn, apply the oil to the skin topically every 3–4 hours for several days.

SAFETY NOTE ...

Severe burns need immediate medical attention. Do not try any home remedy on second- or third-degree burns.

MINOR CUT DISINFECTANT AND HEALING OINTMENT

It is important to disinfect a cut so that bacteria do not cause further, more complicated, infections. Many people turn to alcohol or hydrogen peroxide to disinfect their cuts. This can actually damage the skin, so it is best to follow these steps to ensure proper healing.

Yield: about ½ cup (81 g)

¼ cup (60 ml) olive oil

¼ cup (55 g) coconut oil

1 tbsp (5 g) grated beeswax

½ tsp vitamin E oil

10 drops lavender essential oil

6 drops tea tree oil

3 drops helichrysum (optional)

In a double boiler, melt together the olive oil, coconut oil and grated beeswax. Remove from the burner and allow to cool for a minute or two. Stir in the vitamin E, lavender oil, tea tree oil and helichrysum if you are using it. Pour into a 4-ounce (118-ml) container and allow to set for a few hours. Store in a cool, dry place.

Wash your hands very well before cleaning the wound.

Stop the bleeding by applying pressure with a clean towel or a sterile piece of gauze.

Use sterile tweezers to remove any debris that might be in the wound. You can use alcohol to sterilize your tweezers.

Clean the wound with a mild soap and some warm water.

Apply the healing ointment to promote healthy regrowth of the skin.

To use, place a small amount onto the wound and gently rub in. Repeat as needed.

Cover the wound with a bandage. Change the dressing daily.

SAFETY NOTE ...

See a doctor if the wound becomes inflamed or becomes red around the edges, is warm to the touch, has drainage or swelling, or if you experience an increase in pain.

BRUISES

Bruises are ruptured blood vessels underneath the skin that are caused by impact. The key to healing bruises quickly is to ice them right away. After 48 hours, or after the swelling has gone down, replace the ice pad with a heating pad to speed up the healing process. If you really want to speed up your healing, try this natural remedy.

Yield: 1 tbsp (15 ml)

Cold water

1 tsp (5 ml) witch hazel

2 tsp (10 ml) pure aloe vera gel

2–3 drops lavender essential oil (optional)

Ice Pack (see page 164)

Wet a clean washcloth with cold water and squeeze out any excess. Fold the washcloth in thirds. Add the witch hazel, pure aloe vera gel and lavender essential oil to a small bowl and mix slightly. Pour the mixture onto the washcloth. It doesn't have to absorb fully into the washcloth; you want it to lie on the surface.

Gently place the washcloth, solution side down, onto the bruise. Place an ice pack on top of the washcloth and leave it on for 15–20 minutes. Repeat 2–3 times a day. Adjust this solution for larger bruises by doubling or tripling the witch hazel, pure aloe vera gel and lavender.

Aloe helps heal broken blood vessels under the skin quickly and can help reduce inflammation. Aloe helps disinfect, has antimicrobial and antibacterial properties and fights germs and viruses.

RAZOR BUMPS

When it comes to razor bumps, prevention is your best method. First, exfoliate dead skin cells by brushing your skin with a stiff toothbrush, brush, exfoliating mitt, loofah sponge or moistened pumice stone. Avoid using a pumice stone on your face; it can be too harsh.

Practice good shaving techniques. Use natural conditioners, soaps or gels to moisten the skin before shaving. Always use a sharp razor. Try not to cut too close to the skin. Always move the razor in the direction of the hair growth with short, small movements. Electric clippers can be a better option than razors when trying to prevent razor bumps.

To prevent razor bumps, apply a gel solution right after shaving. Use it 1 or 2 times a day.

Yield: about ¼ cup (61 g)

¼ cup (85 g) pure aloe vera gel

½ tsp raw honey

1–2 drops tea tree oil (optional)

In a small container, combine the pure aloe vera gel, raw honey and tea tree oil, if using. Mix well and pour into a squeezable container. To use, place a small amount onto the freshly shaved area. Allow the area to completely dry. Repeat up to 2 times a day.

WARTS

Warts are a benign growth on the skin that can be incredibly hard to get rid of. They are a viral infection. Warts can spread quickly just by means of shaking someone's hand, using a public keyboard, turning a doorknob or skin-to-skin contact.

Everyone is exposed to this virus at some point in their life, but not everyone gets warts. People with strong immune systems often can fight off the virus before it produces a wart. If you are suffering from warts, consider looking into supplements that support your immune system. A few supplements to consider taking orally are zinc sulfate, turmeric, garlic and olive leaf extract.

Patience is critical when trying to get rid of a wart naturally. You need to tackle the virus, and being persistent with this treatment method is imperative for successful removal.

Yield: about ¼ tsp for paste

Oral zinc sulphate

½ tsp turmeric

Olive oil

1 drop tea tree oil

Adhesive Bandage (page 166)

Pumice stone

Start by taking a quality supplement of zinc sulphate. Zinc can be beneficial for getting rid of warts.

In a small bowl, mix together the turmeric and olive oil to create a thick paste. Add a drop of tea tree oil. Place a small amount of the paste on the wart and cover with an adhesive bandage. Do this in the morning and again in the evening. Every few days, use a pumice stone to file down the wart. Repeat this method until the wart is gone.

Turmeric has been in use for over 4,000 years. It helps heal viral and bacterial infections, inflammation, and research indicates that it can help fight cancer. Turmeric can be taken in capsules, tinctures, cut root or in a fluid extract.

DID YOU KNOW...

Turmeric will stain the skin a yellow color. This is normal. After a few days, the color will dissipate. You can use a pumice stone to remove the yellow skin faster if you like.

SAFETY NOTE...

If you are under 18, pregnant or nursing or are currently on medications, ask your doctor before trying this solution.

SPLINTERS

A splinter is a tiny piece of wood, metal, glass or another foreign material that embeds itself in the skin. There are several methods for removing a stubborn splinter from your skin.

Yield: varies

HYDROGEN PEROXIDE

Hydrogen peroxide

BAKING SODA PASTE

Baking soda

Water

MAGNESIUM SULFATE

Magnesium sulfate (Epsom salt)

ESSENTIAL OILS

1 drop lavender essential oil

1 drop clove essential oil

HYDROGEN PEROXIDE

Place a small amount of hydrogen peroxide in a bowl and soak the splinter for several minutes. This will typically bring the splinter to the surface where it can easily be removed with some tweezers.

BAKING SODA PASTE

Make a paste of baking soda and water. Spread it onto the area that has the splinter. Cover with an adhesive bandage overnight. The next morning, the splinter should have worked its way to the surface. Use tweezers to gently remove it.

MAGNESIUM SULFATE (EPSOM SALT)

Place a small amount of Epsom salt onto the area that has the splinter. Cover with an adhesive bandage. Replace the adhesive bandage and Epsom salt once per day or if the area gets wet. The magnesium sulfate will bring the splinter to the surface, where you can gently remove it from the skin.

ESSENTIAL OILS

Lavender and clove essential oils can be used to push the splinter out of your skin. Place 1 drop of each oil onto the splinter. Wait 10–15 minutes for the splinter to come to the surface. Remove it gently with a pair of tweezers.

CHAFING POWDER

Chafing is when an area of skin becomes sore and irritated from something rubbing against it. It is often caused by clothing that is too tight or too loose, excess, repetitive movement, sensitive skin, weather conditions, sand, dirt or salt (from the beach) or excess body weight. Making your own chafing powder can help relieve irritation and friction.

Yield: about ²/₃ cup (118 g)

½ cup (122 g) arrowroot powder or corn starch

2 tbsp (28 g) bentonite clay

5 drops lavender essential oil (optional)

1–2 drops peppermint essential oil (optional)

Use a container with a shaker cap. Place all the ingredients in the container and gently shake until combined. To use, place a small amount onto your hand and apply to the area in need. Gently spread onto the skin. Repeat as needed.

DID YOU KNOW...

Peppermint essential oil has a cooling effect on the skin. Adding just a drop or two to this solution can really make this a soothing and cooling powder.

This can also be used as a baby powder, but do not use lavender or peppermint on babies. Simply leave the essential oils out and you have a wonderful baby powder. Never sprinkle this powder or any powder next to a baby's face. Apply to your hands, away from the baby and then gently rub into your baby's skin.

POISON IVY AND POISON OAK

Poison ivy and poison oak are Asian and North American plants that, when touched, can cause a red itchy rash. One can get poison ivy or oak from touching any part of either plant, even if the plant is dead. Burning poison ivy or oak in a camp fire can also cause irritation.

Not everyone is allergic to poison ivy or poison oak, but most people will notice some itching and skin irritation within 24 to 48 hours of contact. Bumps and blisters can appear and ooze liquid. The rash can last anywhere from 5 to 12 days.

The rash from poison ivy or poison oak is not contagious. Urushiol, the oily allergen found in poison ivy and poison oak, is what is contagious. When you brush against poison ivy, it is the urushiol that causes the rash. If it remains on your skin or on the clothes that you are wearing, it can spread to others. Always wash your clothing and skin after you come in contact with poison ivy or poison oak to prevent it from spreading to other parts of your body or to another person. Wash clothing (shoes included) in hot water with a detergent that cuts through grease (see recipe on page 50).

Yield: paste: about 1½ tbsp (23 g), bath: varies

1 cup (206 g) + 2 tbsp (26 g) baking soda (divided)

Water

Apple cider vinegar

2–3 drops lavender essential oil (optional)

Mix 1 cup (206 g) of baking soda into a warm bath and soak for 20–30 minutes. Dry completely.

In a small bowl, add 2 tablespoons (26 g [or more if you have a large outbreak]) of baking soda and add enough apple cider vinegar to create a paste similar to a thick pancake batter. The mixture will bubble up; this is normal. Stir in lavender if desired.

Spread the paste over the poison ivy or oak and allow it to dry completely. It will eventually flake. Try to keep it on as long as you can. Once it starts to flake, you can brush it off. It is still working even though you have brushed off the flakes. Repeat as needed.

SAFETY NOTE . . .

Seek medical attention immediately if you experience difficulty breathing, fever, nausea, trouble swallowing, swelling of the face or hands, headache or nausea. If the rash covers more than 25% of your body, see a doctor.

Lavender can help reduce inflammation of the skin and can help heal a burn when applied topically to the skin. It reduces or eliminates swelling, itchy skin and pain.

BEE AND WASP STINGS

Getting stung by a wasp or a bee can hurt! Bees can sting only once, but wasps can sting multiple times. Once you are stung, the venom goes deep under your skin and you can quickly start to experience symptoms. Pain, redness, minor swelling and itching are all signs that you might have been stung. A raised welt might appear where you were stung, and there is often a white area in the middle where the stinger actually went into the skin. There are several remedies that can help reduce the pain of a sting.

Straight, firm edge (e.g., a credit card)

Warm, soapy water

Vinegar

Ice Pack (page 164)

Healing Ointment (page 155)

Anti-Itch Bug Bite Lotion (page 163)

First, if you are stung by a bee or a wasp be sure to remove the stinger. Avoid pinching the stinger out or using tweezers, as these methods can cause the venom to go further into the skin. Instead use a straight, firm edge, such as a credit card, to remove the stinger.

Wash the area with warm soapy water to remove any venom that remains on the surface. Pour a small amount of vinegar onto the bite to stop the stinging. Place an ice pack on the area to reduce the swelling, and apply pressure at the same time.

Apply a small amount of Healing Ointment onto the bite. If the bite begins to itch, apply a small amount of Anti-Itch Bug Bite Lotion to the welt.

The pain from a sting usually disappears within several hours of being stung; however, some people can have life-threatening complications from bee or wasp stings. When the body goes into shock from the venom, it is called anaphylaxis. Seek medical attention immediately if you experience any of the following symptoms after being stung. Do not wait! Going into anaphylaxis can happen very quickly.

Severe swelling of the lips, face, tongue or throat

Hives appear in other areas of the body, outside of where you were stung

Difficulty breathing

Dizziness and lightheadedness

Stomach cramps

Vomiting or nausea

Diarrhea

Fast or slow pulse

ANTI-ITCH BUG BITE LOTION

Bug bites can put a damper on any outdoor activity. Gear yourself up with an anti-itch bug bite lotion that is sure to tackle even the nastiest bug bites.

This lotion is meant to be thick so it can stay on the surface rather than absorb into the skin. That is the magic of this lotion. If you do not want to see grayish-white spots where you apply this lotion, consider putting it on at night and letting it work while you sleep.

Yield: about ⅓ cup or 2 oz (57 g)

2 tbsp (23 g) powdered bentonite clay

1½ tbsp (17 g) calcium carbonate powder

4–5 tbsp (60–75 ml) distilled water

¼ tsp vitamin E oil

15 drops peppermint essential oil (optional)

In a non-metal bowl, add the powdered clay and calcium powder. Add 4 tablespoons (60 ml) of water and work it in well with a wooden spoon or with your hands. Add another tablespoon (15 ml) of water if needed and work it into the clay. You want a soft, wet clay that is still somewhat thick.

Stir in the vitamin E and peppermint essential oil. Transfer the mixture into a squeezable container.

To use, add a small amount of lotion to the bug bite. Do not rub it; let the thick paste fully cover the bug bite. Allow it to fully dry. Repeat as needed.

EXTRA TIP …

It is best to avoid using metal when working with clay since the clay absorbs the metals and becomes less effective. Don't use metal spoons or bowls and don't store your clay products in metal containers.

FLEXIBLE, REUSABLE ICE PACKS

When someone has an injury that requires ice, you either have to deal with bulky ice in a bag that might leak, or you have to use a solid ice pack that has no flexibility.

Flexibility is important, especially if you are trying to ice an elbow, knee or other area that requires that something be draped over it. This ice pack makes a great addition to any do-it-yourself first aid kit.

The key ingredient for this solution is alcohol. Alcohol doesn't fully freeze, and it makes a slush-like substance that is perfect for treating any injury. It is reusable and can be kept in the freezer for a long period of time.

Yield: 1 ice pack

1 quart-size (946 ml) freezer bag (optional: second 1 quart [946 ml] freezer bag for extra protection)

1 cup (237 ml) water

$1/3$ cup (78 ml) 70% rubbing alcohol

3–4 drops food coloring (optional)

With a permanent marker, label the freezer bag "reusable ice pack" and fill with water and alcohol. You can double the bag for extra leak protection. Shake gently and add 3–4 drops of food coloring, if you wish.

Place in the freezer for 12–24 hours before using.

When in need of an ice pack, pull it out and drape it where needed, as the ice pack is flexible and will cover the area. When you are done, return it to the freezer for future use.

REUSABLE HEATING PADS

Heating pads are often needed when an injury occurs. Sure, there are electric heating pads, but you have to always be by an outlet to use them.

Creating a reusable heating pad is very simple. Here are two easy methods.

Yield: 1 heating pad

METHOD 1

1½ cups (316 g) rice

2 clean tube socks

METHOD 2

Felt fabric

Hot glue gun

Hot glue

Rice

METHOD 1

Place the rice in an old, clean tube sock. Close the opening with a knot. Place the filled sock in the other empty sock, putting the knot end in first. Knot the open end of the outer sock.

To use, heat it in the microwave for 45 seconds. Remove it from the microwave to check the temperature. If you'd like it hotter, heat it for an additional 15 seconds. Repeat this step until you get your desired heat. Rice heats up quickly, so be sure to keep an eye on your heating pad. Once it's heated, it is ready for use.

METHOD 2

Purchase a piece of felt of your desired size. It should be large enough to fold over onto itself; only three sides need to be glued. Fold the fabric in half, and with a hot glue gun carefully glue two sides shut, leaving only one side open. Allow to fully dry. Fill with your desired amount of rice and glue the final side shut. Allow to fully dry before using.

To use, heat it in the microwave for 45 seconds. Remove from the microwave to check the temperature. If you'd like it hotter, heat it for an additional 15 seconds. Repeat this step until you get your desired heat. Rice heats up quickly, so be sure to keep an eye on your heating pad. Once it's heated, it is ready for use.

DO-IT-YOURSELF ADHESIVE BANDAGES

Sometimes you get stuck without adhesive bandages and you have to get a little creative. Adhesive bandages aren't hard to make. Before using one, make sure that the area of the wound is cleaned properly and that nothing foreign has gotten into the cut.

Avoid using cotton balls on an open cut, as little pieces of cotton can get stuck in the wound. If you have an allergy to latex, make sure you are not using adhesive tape that contains latex. Always thoroughly clean the wound and put a healing ointment on it (see page 155).

Yield: 1 bandage

Gauze (in a pinch, an all-natural paper towel will work)

Paper tape or adhesive medical tape (or in a pinch other tapes will work)

Fold a piece of gauze into a square large enough to cover the wound. Place the gauze over the wound and use some paper tape, adhesive medical tape or— in a pinch—any tape, to secure the gauze to the wound. Make sure the tape is long enough to properly adhere to the skin. If you have an allergy to adhesives, use a ribbon or string to hold the gauze in place.

BUTTERFLY ADHESIVE BANDAGES (TO HELP CLOSE A WOUND)

Sometimes a cut isn't quite deep enough for stitches, but you still want to pull the smooth edges together for proper healing. The butterfly adhesive bandage is a great way to do this.

Yield: 1 bandage

Adhesive tape ½- to 1-inch wide (13–25-mm) wide

Scissors

Cut a piece of 1-inch (25-mm) adhesive tape about 1 inch (25 mm) in length. Fold it in half so that the non-sticky sides are face-to-face and the sticky sides are on the outside. Cut a notch about one quarter of the way from the folded side up towards the center of the tape, but don't cut all the way to the center so that the cut tape drops out. Repeat this notch on the other side. Leave the cut portions flapping.

Unfold the tape so that the sticky side is facing up. Fold the sticky notch flaps inward so they overlap and create a non-sticky center. This area will have no adhesive and will be placed over the wound. Place the tape on one side of the wound and lay the middle non-adhesive center over the wound. Pull the smooth edges of the wound back together. Place the remaining tape on the other side of the wound to close the cut.

If the wound is long, make several butterfly bandages to properly close the entire wound.

On one side of the tape, cut a triangle about ¼ inch (6 mm) above the folded line towards the center of the tape, being careful not to cut all the way to the center. Repeat to the other side.

Fold the center triangles inward overlapping one another and stick the center pieces together to create a non-sticky center.

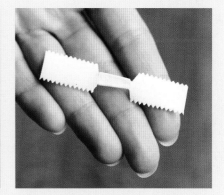

This should close the wound. Make several butterfly bandages depending on the size of the wound.

DIGESTIVE SYSTEM

If your digestive system isn't working properly, a lot of other issues can flare up. One of the most important factors to consider when you are having digestive issues is your diet. Evaluate your diet to see where and how you can improve it. Consider being tested for food allergies, as an allergy can often cause issues for your digestive system.

Signs that your digestive system isn't working as effectively as it could be include gas, bloating and excess belching. If you experience these aliments, consider not drinking out of a straw, not chewing gum and not sucking on hard candy or drinking carbonated beverages. These activities sometimes cause people to swallow air, which can lead to more gas, bloating and belching.

Other digestive issues include constipation, diarrhea and hemorrhoids. In this chapter, I go over ways you can boost your digestive system to conquer these common ailments.

Do you ever get the hiccups? Learn what causes them and what you can do to help yourself and others get rid of them quickly (page 175)!

You can heal your digestive system with time. Discover simple solutions to aid your healing journey throughout this chapter.

CONSTIPATION

Constipation is a condition in which it is difficult to release stool from the body. Symptoms of constipation include infrequent bowel movements (fewer than three stools a week), hard stool, straining to eliminate stool, cramping or abdominal pain and a sensation of blockage or that everything did not come out.

One of the best ways to get rid of constipation is to change your diet. Look for possible food allergies. Explore doing an elimination diet, or see a healthcare provider to pinpoint any allergies to certain foods. Eat more fruits and vegetables and increase your water intake. Eliminate processed foods and fried foods entirely.

One of the most beneficial foods for constipation is celery juice. Celery juice can help someone who has poor digestion. It is nature's natural stool softener and is incredibly good for you.

Yield: 14–16 oz (414–473 ml)

1 head of celery, organic if possible

Cut up the celery into 4-inch (10-cm) pieces. Juice the entire head of celery by running it through a juicer. If you do not have a juicer, use a high-powered blender for about a minute and then strain. One head of celery should yield 14–16 ounces (414–473 ml) of celery juice. It is best to drink celery juice right away.

SAFETY NOTE ...

Talk to a healthcare provider if you are pregnant, nursing or under the age of 18 before trying this method.

DID YOU KNOW...

Celery juice has been known to help fight cancer, lower cholesterol and improve digestion. Celery has diuretic and anti-inflammatory qualities. It improves insomnia, aids with weight loss, eliminates toxins and can increase one's sexual drive.

DIARRHEA

Healthy stool is usually soft but solid. Diarrhea, however, is a condition in which stool comes out in liquid form and occurs more frequently than usual. Common causes of diarrhea include virus, stomach flu, food poisoning, food allergy, parasites, bacterial infection and irritable bowel syndrome (IBS).

Often, diarrhea can be cleared up with a few diet modifications. Chronic diarrhea should always be addressed with your healthcare provider.

During a bout of diarrhea, it is very important to rehydrate your body and replace your electrolytes (page 135). Here are several steps to help rid your body of diarrhea.

ADULTS

Take a good probiotic or digestive enzyme. Probiotics are live bacteria and yeasts that help replenish the good bacteria in your gut. They help fight infection and can aid in getting rid of diarrhea. A lot of food nutrients aren't absorbed properly during diarrhea. Digestive enzymes can help with absorption.

ADULTS AND CHILDREN

Eat more healing foods and avoid the following:

Alcohol, cocoa, chocolate, processed dairy, processed sugar, spicy foods, caffeine and too much fat. Avoid salad greens as these can be rough on your body's digestive system when you have diarrhea.

Always try to stay hydrated with water when you have diarrhea. Coconut water is another good choice because it can replenish your electrolytes—potassium, sodium and magnesium. Bone broths are very nourishing when you are suffering from diarrhea. Foods especially helpful for children are bananas, rice, applesauce, toast and cooked or mashed carrots.

HEALING DRINK FOR DIARRHEA

Yield: 24–30 oz (709–887 g)

½–1 cup (118–237 ml) coconut water

2 bananas

2 large spoonfuls of applesauce

½ cup (small handful) ice

In a blender, add coconut water and the bananas. Top with a few spoonfuls of applesauce and ice and blend until smooth. Sip throughout the day slowly.

HEMORRHOIDS

A hemorrhoid is a swollen blood vessel or group of swollen blood vessels in the rectum and are often referred to as "piles." Common symptoms are bleeding, pain, swelling, itching or irritation and lumps in the anal area. Hemorrhoids can occur internally or externally. External hemorrhoids are located under the skin around the rectum. They tend to be more visible than internal ones and are often more painful.

There are several ways to relieve your symptoms while your hemorrhoids heal:

WITCH HAZEL

Soak a cotton pad in some witch hazel and place it on the area of concern. Let it sit for several minutes before you remove the pad.

ICE

Ice the area that is sore. This can help reduce some of the inflammation.

WARM WATER

Take a warm sitz bath by adding some warm water to a squeeze bottle and gently squirting the area between the rectum and the vulva or scrotum. Bathe regularly in warm water and avoid using soap while healing your hemorrhoids, as this can make them worse.

MOIST TOWELETTES

Avoid using toilet paper, which can irritate the area further. Use moist towelettes that are free of fragrance and dyes.

ALOE VERA

Aloe vera is nature's anti-inflammatory. Dab a little pure aloe vera gel onto the area for a soothing effect.

ESSENTIAL OILS

Add some essential oils diluted in a carrier oil to the area of concern. Commonly used essential oils for hemorrhoids are lavender, tea tree oil and rosemary.

SAFETY NOTE...

Hemorrhoids usually heal on their own within a few weeks. If you experience bleeding, consider seeing a doctor to rule out a more serious condition. If your stool changes colors or becomes very dark, or if you become dizzy or feel faint, seek medical attention immediately.

GAS, BLOATING AND BELCHING

Gas, bloating and belching can be so bothersome. There are natural ways to help relieve these aliments. First, evaluate your diet, since gas, bloating and belching are signs that you have eaten something that hasn't agreed with you. Eat foods that are whole, natural and unprocessed. Stay away from fried foods altogether. Consider trying an elimination diet to rule out any food allergies, or see an allergist for further testing.

Next, stay away from lifestyle choices that can contribute to excess air in your system. Stop chewing gum. Did you know that when you chew gum, you are swallowing air? The excess air can lead to more gas, bloating and belching. Drinking out of a straw, sucking on candy and drinking carbonated beverages can also cause you to swallow air.

PROBIOTICS AND DIGESTIVE ENZYMES

Sometimes gas, bloating and belching can happen when you have the wrong bacteria in your digestive system. Restore your healthy good bacteria by taking a quality probiotic daily.

One of the best ways to help absorb nutrients and break down the foods that you eat is to take digestive enzymes before each meal.

Slow down when you eat. Consuming food too quickly can cause a long list of problems.

CELERY JUICE

Many people who suffer from gas, bloating and belching need more hydrochloric acid in their system. Consider juicing 1 head of celery every morning and drink the juice on an empty stomach.

Cut up the celery into 4-inch (10-cm) pieces. Juice the entire head of celery by running it through a juicer. If you do not have a juicer, you can blend it in a high-powered blender for about a minute and then strain. One head of celery should yield 14–16 ounces (414–473 ml) of celery juice. It is best to drink celery juice right away.

MINT

Mint can be very beneficial for your digestive system. Peppermint tea can be an easy way to get mint into your diet. Simply sip on a cup of peppermint tea before your meal and even during the meal, if you like. You can make fresh peppermint tea if you have access to peppermint. Simply cut a handful and steep it in hot water for 20 minutes. Remove the leaves and add honey if desired.

(continued)

GAS, BLOATING AND BELCHING (CONT.)

PARSLEY

Ever wonder why there is a sprig of parsley on your plate when you dine in a restaurant? It's because parsley is incredibly effective for reducing bloating, gas and belching. Eat a small sprig of raw parsley right after dinner, or make a tea by putting a handful into some hot water and letting it steep for 20 minutes. Remove and add honey if desired.

FENNEL SEEDS

You can reduce belching simply by chewing on a ½ teaspoon of fennel seeds after a meal. You can also chew caraway, celery or anise seeds. Some people find it more effective to grind 1 teaspoon (3 g) of the seeds into a fine powder and add it to 8 ounces (237 ml) of warm water. Stir and drink. You can add honey and lemon if you desire.

A sprig of parsley often garnishes a dinner plate, but many don't realize that it is there to serve a purpose. Parsley helps relieve bloating, indigestion and gas. It also helps you digest food and draws out excess water from the abdomen. So the next time you get a sprig of parsley on your dinner plate, do your body a favor and eat it.

HICCUPS

A hiccup is an involuntary spasm of the diaphragm that results when an inhale of breath is stopped by the vocal cords or glottis suddenly closing. This results in a sound that resembles a cough, or more commonly, a hiccup.

Several factors that may cause someone to get the hiccups: eating too quickly or too much, drinking an excessive amount of alcohol, swallowing too much air, smoking, drinking something that is too cold or too hot, drinking carbonated beverages, excitement and stress.

A simple distraction can help get rid of the hiccups. Ask the person with the hiccups what they had for breakfast yesterday, or ask them about their favorite meal. Don't tell them why you are asking; the distraction itself is sometimes just what someone needs.

Another effective method is to press down on the tragus of both ears at the same time while simultaneously drinking a glass of water through a straw. (The tragus is the small ridge on the outside of the ear canal that you gently press to plug your ears.) Do not put anything in the ear canal.

SAFETY NOTE ...

Hiccups usually go away on their own within a few minutes. Sometimes they can last several hours. If your hiccups last longer than a few days, it is best to seek out medical attention to rule out more serious problems.

EMOTIONAL AND PAIN SUPPORT

When you need a little emotional and pain support, one of the best places to turn to is nature. Nature actually provides us with many healing tools; we just need to know where to look.

In this chapter, learn how nature can help with sleep (page 183), anxiety (page 185), seasonal depression (page 182) and pain (page 180). With a few ingredients that come right from the earth, you can find relief fast.

Did you know that you can ease PMS and menstrual cramps with herbs and spices (page 178)? Red raspberry leaf, chamomile, nettle leaf, peppermint, oregano and chaste tree berry are all great healing herbs. Cinnamon, cloves and nutmeg are great spices for treating PMS and menstrual cramps.

Insomnia can be treated with the root of one plant and the leaves of another. These two plants have been used for insomnia for over 1000 years! On page 183, you will discover which two plants can help you get a good night's sleep.

Did you know that soaking in a detox bath can help with emotional and pain support? Our bodies are overloaded every day with toxins and impurities that make us feel less than great. Detoxing your body on a regular basis can really do wonders for your health. Learn how to properly detox in a bath on page 181.

Let a few of nature's treasures help you.

PMS AND MENSTRUAL CRAMPS

Premenstrual syndrome (PMS) is an imbalance of hormones linked to the menstrual cycle. PMS typically starts about 5–7 days before the menstrual flow and will slowly subside as the flow starts. Symptoms of PMS include headaches, acne, breast tenderness, bloating, fatigue, moodiness, weight gain, back pain, restlessness, irritability, anxiety, cramping and food cravings.

HERBAL TEAS FOR PMS AND MENSTRUAL CRAMPS

Several teas can help reduce, if not eliminate, PMS and menstrual cramps. Red raspberry leaf, chamomile tea, nettle leaf tea, peppermint tea and chaste tree berry tea are all great choices.

Add the following to any of the teas for even more healing results.

Cut a few slices of ginger (peeled, about ½ inch [13 mm] thick) and add them to the tea with a little raw honey and a few slices of lemon. Let them steep with the tea for 10–15 minutes, then strain and drink.

Oregano has also been known to help eliminate cramps. Add about 1 teaspoon (0.5 g) dried oregano or 3 teaspoons (2.5 g) fresh oregano to 1 cup (237 ml) boiling water and allow to steep for 15–20 minutes. Strain, add some honey, lemon and ginger if desired, and drink.

Cinnamon, cloves and nutmeg are great spices for PMS and menstrual cramps. Add ¼ teaspoon of any of these spices to a tea and stir to blend.

If you suffer from PMS and menstrual cramps, consider evaluating your diet. PMS can be triggered by a lack of vitamins and minerals, and certain lifestyle choices. Start working on a few of these lifestyle choices to see if they can help relieve your symptoms.

Consider eliminating chemicals from your diet by purchasing organic food whenever possible. Add more leafy greens to your diet, and eat plenty of fruits. Stay hydrated with fresh lemon water throughout the day. Eliminate processed foods. Avoid processed sugar and table salts; instead, use natural sweeteners like raw honey and pure maple syrup, and replace your table salts with natural sea salts. Eliminate artificial sweeteners, preservatives, natural flavors and artificial colors from your diet. Avoid alcohol and caffeinated beverages. Avoid inflammatory foods like grain-based foods, dairy, vegetable oils and factory-raised meats.

Eliminate daily toxins in your home by following some of the solutions in the Household Cleaning section on page 57. Exercise regularly and work on ways to manage your stress. Yoga and meditation are great for reducing stress. Get enough sleep.

Consider supplementing your diet with magnesium, calcium citrate and evening primrose oil, and take a good multivitamin. Consider taking a good probiotic.

Common herbs found in your kitchen can actually help eliminate menstrual cramps. Add a little ground cinnamon, cloves or nutmeg to a soothing cup of chamomile tea and watch your cramps disappear.

NATURE'S PAIN RELIEF

Nature makes an all-natural pain killer called corydalis. Corydalis is a perennial plant that grows in the northern parts of China, Japan, Russia and Africa. This plant is in the same family as the opium poppy plant. Corydalis root has been used for pain in Chinese medicine for centuries. It is not addictive, and it doesn't have the side effects of today's pharmaceutical pain killers.

Corydalis can be purchased in supplement form or in concentrated granules. It is used to treat chronic pain, nerve pain, inflammation and menstrual cramps.

Corydalis granules provide the quickest way to get relief from pain. It is often made into a tea that dissolves easily in hot water.

Yield: 1 cup (237 ml)

8 oz (237 ml) hot water

¼ tsp corydalis granules (or according to package directions)

1 lemon wedge

1–2 tsp (5–10 ml) raw local honey

Boil water and pour into a mug. Add the corydalis granules and stir until dissolved. Add a slice of lemon and a few spoonfuls of honey.

Corydalis is bitter by nature. If you feel this tea is too bitter for you, simply add the corydalis granules to 1 ounce (30 ml) warm water and dissolve. Drink quickly in one to two swallows.

SAFETY NOTE ...

Always speak to a healthcare provider before taking any herb or supplement. Children and women who are pregnant or nursing should not take or use corydalis.

DETOX BATH

Have you ever taken a detox bath? One might ask, what do we need to detox from? Our bodies are overloaded every day with toxins and impurities, which can make us feel less than great.

Detoxing on a regular basis can really do wonders for your health. One of the best ingredients to use for detoxing is Epsom salt.

Epsom salt dissolves into magnesium and sulfate when added to water. Many of us are deficient in magnesium. One of the quickest ways to replenish magnesium is by absorbing it through the skin.

Consider a detox bath to help relieve arthritis pain, muscle pain, fibromyalgia, insomnia, psoriasis and exhaustion.

Yield: varies

1½ cups (270 g) Epsom salt

1 cup (206 g) baking soda

5 drops lavender essential oil (optional)

5 drops eucalyptus essential oil (optional)

Fill a bathtub with warm water. Dissolve the Epsom salt and baking soda into the bath. Add your essential oils of choice. Immerse your whole body from the neck down. Soak for 20–30 minutes. Do not use commercial shampoos, conditioners or soaps in a detox bath, since these often contain toxins that can be absorbed by the skin. Slowly get out of the bath. Do not rinse, but gently dry yourself off. Drink plenty of water after a detox bath to help flush out the impurities. Repeat this bath 1–3 times a week.

Many of us are deficient in magnesium. Every cell in our body needs magnesium to function. You can help replenish magnesium by adding Epsom salt to your bath. This can help relieve arthritis pain, muscle pain, insomnia and exhaustion.

EXTRA TIP...

Do not use Epsom salt or baking soda in a hot tub or a whirlpool bath. If your bathtub has jets, do not turn them on or run them while taking a detox bath.

SEASONAL DEPRESSION

Seasonal depression, also called seasonal affective disorder (SAD), is a form of depression caused by a change of seasons. It starts around the same time of year, year after year.

Symptoms of seasonal depression include sadness, depression, low energy, sleep issues, weight changes (gain or loss), feelings of anxiousness and irritability and loss of enjoyment of activities that were once enjoyable.

There are several natural remedies for treating seasonal depression:

ESSENTIAL OILS

Diffuse essential oils into your home that are good for depression. Common essential oils used for depression are lemon, frankincense, lavender, bergamot, eucalyptus and grapefruit.

SUPPLEMENTS

Certain supplements can help ease seasonal depression. A few natural supplements that might help relieve seasonal depression symptoms are St. John's wort, SAMe, melatonin, turmeric, vitamin B-12, vitamin D, vitamin C, omega-3 fatty acids and good-quality probiotics.

OTHER REMEDIES FOR SEASONAL DEPRESSION

Seasonal depression often happens in the winter months when sunlight is lacking. Consider some light therapy during these gray days. Quality light therapy lamps can easily be found online.

Dawn simulators are alarm clocks that wake you up by gradually increasing light in the room to simulate the sun rising. Look for a dawn simulator that uses full-spectrum light, which simulates natural sunlight.

Sit near a sunny window whenever possible. If the sun is out, spend the day outdoors.

Exercise can reduce stress and anxiety and improve your mood. Yoga and meditation are great exercises for relaxation.

When dealing with seasonal depression, it is important to take care of yourself. Try to get out and socialize. Schedule a trip to a sunny destination if possible. Try to do things that bring you joy and peace. If you feel you need to talk to someone, schedule an appointment with a qualified counselor.

INSOMNIA

Getting a good night's sleep is so important for overall health. When insomnia strikes, you want to have something on hand that can get you back to sleep fast. One of the best ways to treat insomnia is with herbs, specifically valerian and lemon balm.

Valerian is an herb that has sedative qualities. People have used it for over 1,000 years. It is commonly used to treat anxiety, insomnia, nervousness, headaches, migraines, stomach cramps and menstrual cramps.

Lemon balm is a calming herb in the mint family. It has been in use since the Middle Ages. Common uses for lemon balm are healing cold sores, calming nerves, reducing pain, treating colds, fighting the flu, promoting healthy sleep and helping with chronic fatigue syndrome.

You can get lemon balm and valerian in tinctures, capsules, teas or fresh plants.

Follow the instructions on the label for the proper dosage.

You can buy a product with lemon balm leaf extract and valerian root extract already mixed together. Look for a product that has 160 mg to 320 mg valerian root extract and 80 mg to 150 mg lemon balm extract. Take the recommended dosage 30 minutes before bedtime for best results. Valerian may take a few weeks to build up in your system before it works.

(continued)

INSOMNIA (CONT.)

EXTRA TIP ...

Valerian naturally has a very strong, unpleasant odor. When purchasing, look for an odorless variety.

SAFETY NOTES ...

Always talk to qualified healthcare provider before taking any new medicines or herbal supplements. Do not take if under 18, pregnant or nursing.

Talk to your healthcare provider if you are taking this sleep aid for more than 30 days.

Do not operate a vehicle or heavy machinery while taking these herbs. Do not drink alcohol.

Lemon balm is an herb in the mint family that is commonly used to treat anxiety. Valerian is an herb thats been in use for over 1,000 years and has sedative qualities. Combined these two herbs make a great solution to treat insomnia.

ANXIETY

Anxiety is a feeling of stress, fear, worry, nervousness or tension. It is usually temporary, but sometimes it persists, becoming an anxiety disorder. If you or a loved one deal with anxiety on a regular basis, you probably know how dramatically anxiety can affect one's life. If anxiety is part of your everyday life, consider seeking medical help. If your anxiety is only occasional, here are a few tips for relieving it naturally.

Evaluate your diet. Anxiety is often caused by an underlying issue. Consider putting yourself on an elimination diet to investigate food allergies or sensitivities. Eat often and stay hydrated. Avoid alcohol and caffeinated beverages, which can worsen anxiety. Get regular exercise. Consider a relaxing form of exercise like yoga or meditation. A lack of sleep can cause more stress, so try to get at least 8 hours of sleep a night.

Practice breathing techniques that help reduce tension and stress. Take deep breaths and let go of the air slowly through your mouth. Practice the 4-7-8 breathing exercise: Completely exhale all the air out through your mouth. Through your nose, take a breath in for 4 seconds. Hold your breath for 7 seconds then slowly release the air through your mouth for 8 seconds. Repeat this process 3 more times.

Lemon balm (*Melissa officinalis*) is an herb in the mint family that can be helpful for anxiety. It can be found in a health food store or online. You can get lemon balm in a tincture, capsules, topical creams, tea or from a fresh plant.

Follow the instructions on the label for the proper dosage. Common dosages are:

Capsules: 300–500 mg powdered lemon balm, 2 times a day.

Tea: ¼ teaspoon to 1 teaspoon (0.5 g) of dried lemon balm or 2–3 sprigs of fresh lemon balm, 4 times a day. Steep in hot water for 15–20 minutes, strain and drink.

Tincture (alcohol-free, preferably): 20 drops in 2 ounces (60 ml) water 2–5 times per day.

Topical: Topical creams are used more for cold sores, not for anxiety. See Cold Sores on page 121.

SAFETY NOTE...

Always talk to a qualified healthcare provider before taking any new medicines or herbal supplements. Do not take if under 18, pregnant or nursing. Children can take lemon balm topically, but speak to a pediatrician for proper dosage.

REFERENCES

1—DARKEN HAIR NATURALLY (PAGE 109):

"Henna," last modified 2016. https://www.mountainroseherbs.com/products/henna/profile.

2—PINKEYE (PAGE 112):

"Natural Remedies for Pinkeye," last modified Jul 18, 2016. http://www.drwhitaker.com/natural-remedies-for-pink-eye.

3—EXCESS WAX REMOVAL FROM EARS (PAGE 113):

"Earwax Home Treatment," last modified Jun 4, 2014. http://www.webmd.com/a-to-z-guides-earwax-home-treatment.

4—SWIMMER'S EAR (PAGE 114):

"Swimmer's ear," last modified May 5, 2016. http://www.mayoclinic.org/diseases-conditions/swimmers-ear/manage/ptc-20201568.

5—COLD SORES (PAGE 121):

"Lysine," last modified 2016. http://www.webmd.com/vitamins-supplements/ingredientmono-237-lysine.aspx?activeingredientid=237&activeingredientname=lysine.

6— ACNE CONTROL MASK (PAGE 125):

"Zinc levels in patients with acne vulgaris," last modified Feb 21, 2011. http://www.jtad.org/2007/3/jtad71302a.pdf-

7—FLU (PAGE 132):

"Elderberry Fights Flu Symptoms," last modified Dec 22, 2003, http://www.webmd.com/cold-and-flu/news/20031222/elderberry-fights-flu-symptoms.

8—HEARTBURN, ACID REFLUX AND GERD (PAGE 133):

"Apple Cider Vinegar Benefits for Acid Reflux," last modified Apr 26, 2015, http://www.livestrong.com/article/478034-apple-cider-vinegar-benefits-for-acid-reflux/.

9—JOCK ITCH (PAGE 146):

"Jock Itch," last modified Mar 12, 2014, http://www.webmd.com/men/tc/jock-itch-topic-overview.

10—PLAQUE PSORIASIS TREATMENT (PAGE 151):

"What is Psoriasis?," last modified 2015, https://www.psoriasis.com/what-is-psoriasis.

11—ROSACEA TREATMENT (PAGE 153):

"Zinc Treatment for Rosacea," last modified Nov 9, 2015, http://www.livestrong.com/article/363187-zinc-treatment-for-rosacea/.

12—MINOR CUT DISINFECTANT AND HEALING OINTMENT (PAGE 155):

"How to Treat Minor Cuts and Scrapes," last modified Aug 26, 2015, http://www.webmd.com/allergies/cuts-scrapes.

13—WARTS (PAGE 158):

"Oral zinc sulphate in the treatment of recalcitrant viral wars: randomized placebo-controlled clinical trial," last modified Mar 2002, http://www.ncbi.nlm.nih.gov/pubmed/11952542.

14 – BEE AND WASP STINGS (PAGE 162):

"Are You Allergic to Insect Stings?," last modified Feb 25, 2016, http://www.webmd.com/allergies/guide/insect-stings.

15—DIARRHEA (PAGE 171):

"Diarrhea," last modified 2016, http://www.drweil.com/drw/u/ART00344/diarrhea.html.

16—HEMORRHOIDS (PAGE 172):

"Hemorrhoids Treatment," last modified 2016, http://www.drweil.com/drw/u/ART03032/Hemorrhoids.html.

17—GAS, BLOATING AND BELCHING (PAGE 173):

"How to Relieve Gas Naturally," last modified Aug 17, 2016, http://www.drdavidwilliams.com/how-to-relieve-gas-naturally/.

18—HICCUPS (PAGE 175):

"Hiccups," last modified Sep 21, 2011, http://www.drdougwillen.com/hiccups/.

19—PMS AND MENSTRUAL CRAMPS (PAGE 178):

"Premenstrual syndrome (PMS) fact sheet," last modified Dec 23, 2014, http://www.womenshealth.gov/publications/our-publications/fact-sheet/premenstrual-syndrome.html.

20—NATURE'S PAIN RELIEF (PAGE 180):

"Natural Pain Killers That Work, Pt 1," last modified Jan 28, 2014, http://www.doctoroz.com/episode/natural-pain-killers-work.

21—DETOX BATH (PAGE 181):

"Why Take an Epsom Salt Bath?," last modified Jul 15, 2015, http://www.webmd.com/a-to-z-guides/Epsom-salt-bath.

22—SEASONAL DEPRESSION (PAGE 182):

"Seasonal affective disorder (SAD)," last modified Sept 12, 2014, http://www.mayoclinic.org/diseases-conditions/seasonal-affective-disorder/basics/definition/con-20021047.

23—SEASONAL DEPRESSION (PAGE 182):

Tools, aroma. *Modern Essentials: A Contemporary Guide to the Therapeutic Use of Essential Oils.* 5th ed. Aroma tools. 2013.

24—SEASONAL DEPRESSION (PAGE 182):

"Dawn simulation vs. bright light in seasonal affective disorder, Treatment effects and subjective preference," last modified Jul 15, 2015, http://www.ncbi.nlm.nih.gov/pubmed/25885065.

25—INSOMNIA (PAGE 183):

"Valerian," last modified Jun 26, 2014, http://umm.edu/health/medical/altmed/herb/valerian.

26—INSOMNIA (PAGE 183):

"Lemon Balm," last modified Jan 2, 2015, http://umm.edu/health/medical/altmed/herb/lemon-balm.

27—INSOMNIA (PAGE 183):

"Lemon Balm," last modified Mar 19, 2014, http://www.drweil.com/drw/u/REM00045/Lemon-Balm-Dr-Weils-Herbal-Remedies.html.

28—ANXIETY (PAGE 185):

"Breathing: Three Exercises," last modified 2016, http://www.drweil.com/drw/u/ART00521/three-breathing-exercises.html.

29—ANXIETY (PAGE 185):

"Tips to Manage Anxiety and Stress," last modified 2016, http://www.adaa.org/tips-manage-anxiety-and-stress.

30—ANXIETY (PAGE 185):

"Lemon balm," last modified Jan 2, 2015. http://umm.edu/health/medical/altmed/herb/lemon-balm.

ACKNOWLEDGMENTS

To my girls and my husband David, thank you for always believing in me. I couldn't have done this without you. My heart is filled with love!

To Nikki, Jay, Hilary and Mom, thank you for supporting me my entire life and always being my safe landing spot.

Thank you Dad, for sharing your love of nature and for helping me find my entrepreneurial spirit at such a young age. You are missed and loved daily.

To Linda, thank you for constantly putting vinegar in front of me and reminding me again and again—"Have you tried vinegar yet?"

To Sandy, thank you for understanding and seeing my vision before I even had a chance to form it entirely in my head. And to Julie, thank you for testing my solutions without me having to ask.

To Lauren, our chance meeting on the beach was no mistake. Thank you for all of the camera talk and for taking my head shots.

To Liz and Will, thank you for taking a chance on me. It has been such a pleasure working with you and your incredible team at Page Street Publishing.

And to that ambitious 9-year-old girl who dreamed big after writing her first book on orange construction paper with colored pencils, and said out loud, "When I grow up, I'm going to be an author!": We finally did it!

ABOUT THE AUTHOR

Halle Cottis is very passionate about living a natural lifestyle. She grew up in a rural community where the Amish still exist, and the charm of how things once were done is still present. At a young age, she adopted these simpler techniques for a natural lifestyle and still uses these solutions in her day-to-day life.

She is the founder of Whole Lifestyle Nutrition, where she blogs about allergy-friendly recipes, natural solutions and health and lifestyle tips. She is a Holistic Life Coach and her mission is to help others find their way to a more healthy and natural lifestyle.

Halle resides in Florida with her husband and three beautiful daughters. In her free time she enjoys nature walks, gardening, photography, boating, fishing and relaxing on the beach with friends and family.

INDEX

A

acid reflux, heartburn and GERD relief, 133

acne control mask, 125

adhesive bandages, 166, 167

air freshener spray, 71

allergies, 123

almond oil, 13

aloe vera, 13

ant control, 87

anxiety, 185

arrowroot powder, 14

Asian lady beetles control, 82–83

athlete's foot, treatment for, 145

B

bad breath control and mouthwash, 119

baking soda, 14, 23, 49

balm, healing, for muscles and joints, 147

bathroom

air freshener, 71

detox bath, 181

granite countertop cleaner, 38

grout cleaner, 29

hard water deposit remover, 30

mirror cleaner, 31

mold and mildew cleaners, 26

potpourri, simmering, 74

scouring powder, 28

soap-scum cleaner, 27

soft-scrub cleaners, 25

toilet cleaner, 24

bed bugs, eliminating, 88

bee and wasp stings, 162

beeswax pellets, 14

bentonite clay powder, 14

bleach alternative, 51

blender, high-speed, 19

blood stain removal, 55

body wash for sensitive skin, 138

borax, 14

bruises, 156

bug bite, anti-itch ointment, 163

bug spray and patio diffuser, 94

burns, minor, 154

C

calcium carbonate powder, 14

candles, no-wax, 69, 73

canker sores, 120

car cleaners, 98–99

carpet deodorizer, 70

carpet stain remover, 61

castile liquid soap, 14

cast iron skillet cleaner, 44

castor oil, 15

celery juice, 135

coconut juice, 135

coconut oil, 15

colloidal silver, 15

containers, 18–19

centipedes and millipedes, eliminating, 90

chafing powder, 160

chest, throat and immune system

cough and sore throat syrup, 129

electrolytes, restoring, 135

flu, 132

heartburn, acid reflux and GERD, 133

nasal decongestant rinse, 128

stomachache, 134

vapor rub, 130

cigarette smoke odor remover, 62

cockroaches, eliminating, 84

coconut oil and gum care, 115

coffee pot and coffee machine cleaner, 43

cold sores, 121

constipation, remedy for, 170

copper, solid, cleaner, 46

cough and sore throat syrup, 129

cuts, minor, disinfectant for, 155

cutting board cleaner, 47

D

dandruff control, 110

degreaser, 39

deodorants, body, 140, 141

deodorizers

air freshener spray, 71

Asian lady beetle scent, 83

bathroom air freshener, 72

candles, no-wax, 69, 73

car, 77

carpet, 70

fish and bacon odor, 78

garlic and onion odor, 79

refrigerator, 75

spray, easy, 140

trash can, 76

washing machine, 53

detergent

dishwasher, 35

laundry, 50, 51

detox bath, 181

diarrhea, 171

diatomaceous earth, 15, 28, 81, 85

digestive complaints
    constipation, 170
    diarrhea, 171
    gas, bloating and belching, 173–74
    hemorrhoids, 172
    hiccups, 175
dish soap, lemon, 34
dishwasher detergent, 35
disinfectant cleaner, all-purpose, 36
drain clog remover, 42
Dr. Bronner's Sal Suds, 15, 49

E

ear care
    swimmer's, treatment for, 114
    wax removal from, 113
eczema treatment, 150
electrolytes, restoring, 135
emotional support
    anxiety, 185
    insomnia, 183–84
    PMS and menstrual cramps, 178–79
    seasonal depression, 182–83
essential oils, 16
    air-freshener combinations, 71
    germ-fighting, 139
    hair care, 105
    helichrysum, 153
    lip care, 122
    melaleuca, 26, 110
    for stomachache, 134
ethanol alcohol, 16
eye care
    pinkeye, 112
    stye, 111

F

fabric softener, scented, 52
fabric upholstery cleaner, 63
face wash and toner, foaming, 124
fleas, eliminating, 85
floor cleaner
    general, 59
    for wood floors, 60
flowers, fresh-cut, food for, 64
flu, 132
foot odor, 144
fragrances, 69
fruit flies, eliminating, 86
fruits, used for deodorizers, 66
furniture, leather, cleaner, 66

G

garbage disposal cleaner, 41
gardens
    pesticide, natural, 96
    weed killer, 95
garlic and onion odor, 79
gas, bloating and belching, 173–74
GERD, acid reflux and heartburn relief, 133
gingivitis, 115
glass bottles, 19
granite countertop cleaner, 38
grill cleaner, heavy-duty, 97
grout cleaner, 29

H

hair care
    dandruff control, 110
    darkening, 109
    head lice, 106
    lightening, 108
    nourishing mask for, 107
    shampoo, dry, 105
    for stomachache, 134

hand care
    lotion, creamy, 142
    sanitizer, 139
    wash, foaming, 138
hard water deposit remover, 30
headaches and migraine, 104
head lice, 106
health, common problems with
    acne control mask, 125
    allergies, relief from, 123
    bad breath control,
    canker sores, 120
    cold sores, 121
    cough and sore throat syrup, 129
    electrolytes, restoring, 135
    face wash, foaming, 124
    flu, 132
    gingivitis, 115
    headaches and migraines, 104
    heartburn, acid reflux and GERD relief, 133
    lip balm, healing, 122
    nasal decongestant rinse, 128
    shampoo, dry, 105
    stomachache, 134
    swimmer's ear, 114
    toothache relief, 116
    vapor rub, 130
    wax removal from ears, 113
    whitening teeth, 117
heartburn, acid reflux and GERD relief, 133
heating pad, reusable, 165
hemorrhoids, 172
hiccups, 175
honey, qualities of, 107, 125, 129, 134
hornets and wasps, 89
household cleaning
    carpet stain remover, 61
    cigarette smoke odor remover, 62
    fabric upholstery cleaner, 63

floor cleaner, general, 59

floor cleaner for wood floors, 60

flowers, food for, 64

furniture, leather, cleaner, 66

label and sticky residue remover, 60

screen, television and electronic, cleaner, 67

wall cleaner for crayon and pencil marks, 65

window cleaning, streakless, 58

hydrogen peroxide, 16, 23, 36, 57

I

ice packs, flexible and reusable, 164

ingredients, natural

equipment for, 18–19

list of, 13–17

recycling containers, 11–19

insomnia, 183–84

isopropyl alcohol, 16

J

jock itch, 146

jojoba oil, 16

K

kitchen cleaners

cast iron skillet cleaner, 44

coffee pot and coffee machine cleaner, 43

copper, solid, cleaner, 46

cutting board cleaner, 47

degreaser, 39

disinfectant cleaner, all-purpose, 36

dishwasher detergent, 35

drain clog remover, 42

fish and bacon odor remover, 78

garlic and onion odor remover, 70

garbage disposal cleaner, 41

granite countertop cleaner, 38

lemon dish soap, 34

microwave oven cleaner, 40

oven cleaner, 41

silver and tarnish cleaner, 45

sponge odor, eliminating, 39

stainless steel cleaner, 37

L

label and sticky residue remover, 60

laundry cleaners

blood stain removal, 55

detergent, liquid, 51

detergent, powdered, 50

fabric softener, scented, 52

lemon bleach alternative, 51

stain removal, 55

towels, sour, cleaning of, 54

washing machine deodorizer, 53

lemons

bleach alternative, 51

essential oil, 65

kitchen cleaning, 33, 40

oil, 57

lice, head, 106

lip balm, healing, 122

liquid castile soap, 57

lotion, creamy, 142

M

mice, control of, 91

microfiber cloths, 18

microwave oven cleaner, 40

migraine headache, 104

mirror cleaner, 31

mold and mildew cleaners, 26

mouthwash, and bad breath control, 119

N

nasal decongestant rinse, 128

O

odor removal

cigarette smoke, 62

fish and bacon odor remover, 78

garlic and onion odor remover, 79

sour towel smell, 54

onion and garlic odor remover, 79

outdoor spaces

bug spray and patio diffuser, 94

car de-icer, natural, 99

car wash soap, 98

grill cleaner, heavy-duty, 97

pesticide, natural garden, 96

screen cleaner, 97

wax for cars, 98

weed killer, 95

oven cleaner, 41

P

pain relief, nature's, 180

pest control

ant control, 87

Asian lady beetles, 82–83

bed bugs, 88

centipedes and millipedes, 90

cockroaches, 84

fleas, 85

fruit flies, 86

hornets and wasps, 89

mice, 91

prevention, 81

pinkeye, 112

plaque psoriasis, 151

PMS and menstrual cramps, 178–79

poison ivy and poison oak, 161

potpourri, 72, 74

R

razor bumps, 157
reed diffuser for air freshener, 72
refrigerator deodorizer, 75
rosacea, 152–53

S

salt, 16, 33
scouring powder, 28
screen, television and electronic, cleaner, 67
screen, window, cleaner, 97
scrubbing brush, nylon, 18
seasonal depression, 182–83
shampoo, dry, 105
shea butter, 17
silver and tarnish cleaner, 45
sinus headache, 104
skin care and health conditions
　　adhesive bandages, 166
　　athlete's foot, 145
　　bee and wasp stings, 162
　　body wash for sensitive skin, 138
　　bruises, 156
　　bug bite, anti-itch ointment, 163
　　burns, minor, 154
　　chafing powder, 160
　　cuts, minor, disinfectant for, 155
　　deodorant spray, 140
　　eczema 150
　　foot odor, 144
　　hand wash, foaming, 138
　　hand sanitizer, 139
　　healing balm, sore muscles and joint pain, 147
　　ice packs, flexible and reusable, 164
　　jock itch, 146
　　lotion, creamy, 142
　　plaque psoriasis, 151

　　poison ivy and poison oak, 161
　　razor bumps, 157
　　rosacea treatment, 152–53
　　splinters, 159
　　sunscreen, 143
soap flakes, pure, 16
soap-scum cleaner, 27
soft-scrub cleaners, 25
sore throat and cough syrup, 129
splinters, 159
sponge odor, eliminating, 39
sponges, 18
spray bottles, 18
stainless steel cleaner, 37
stomachache, 134
stye, treatment for, 111
sunscreen, 143
warts, 158

T

teeth
　　gingivitis treatment, 115
　　mouthwash and bad breath control, 119
　　oil pulling, 115
　　toothache relief, 116
　　toothpaste, remineralizing, 118
　　whitening, 117
tension headache, 104
toilet cleaner, 24
toilet paper roll, scented, 72
toothbrush, old, for cleaning, 18
toothpaste, remineralizing, 118
towels, sour, cleaning, 54
trash can deodorizer, 76

U

upholstery, fabric, cleaner, 63

V

vapor rub, 130
vegetable glycerin, 17
vinegar, distilled white, 15, 23, 49
vitamin E oil, 17
vodka, as cleaner, 57

W

wall cleaner for crayon and pencil marks, 65
warts, treatment for, 158
washing machine deodorizer, 53
washing soda, 17, 49
weed killer, 95
whitening for teeth, 117
window cleaning, streakless, 58
witch hazel, 17

Z

zinc oxide powder and zinc sulfate, 17